Goldee's
BAR-B-Q

JALEN HEARD, LANE MILNE & JONNY WHITE

WITH LISA FAIN

A COOKBOOK

PHOTOGRAPHY BY WILL MILNE

UNIVERSITY OF TEXAS PRESS AUSTIN

Publication of this work was made possible in part by support from the J. E. Smothers Sr. Memorial Foundation and the National Endowment for the Humanities.

Printed in China
First edition, 2025

♾ The paper used in this book meets the minimum requirements of ANSI/NISO Z39.48-1992 (R1997) (Permanence of Paper).

LIBRARY OF CONGRESS CATALOGING-IN-PUBLICATION DATA

Names: Heard, Jalen, author. | Milne, Lane, author. | White, Jonny, author. | Fain, Lisa, author. | Milne, Will, photographer.
Title: Goldee's Bar-B-Q : a cookbook / Jalen Heard, Lane Milne, and Jonny White with Lisa Fain; photography by Will Milne.
Description: First edition. | Austin : University of Texas Press, 2025. | Series: Jack and Doris Smothers series in Texas history, life, and culture | Includes index.
Identifiers: LCCN 2024049457 (print) | LCCN 2024049458 (ebook)
ISBN 978-1-4773-3202-3 (hardcover)
ISBN 978-1-4773-3203-0 (PDF)
ISBN 978-1-4773-3204-7 (ePub)
Subjects: LCSH: Barbecuing—Texas—Fort Worth. | Cooking, American—Southwestern style. | Goldee's Bar-B-Q (Restaurant : Fort Worth, Tex.) | LCGFT: Cookbooks.
Classification: LCC TX840.B3 H3945 2025 (print) | LCC TX840.B3 (ebook) | DDC 641.7/6097645315—dc23/eng/20241205
LC record available at https://lccn.loc.gov/2024049457
LC ebook record available at https://lccn.loc.gov/2024049458

doi:10.7560/332023

THE UNIVERSITY OF TEXAS PRESS GRATEFULLY ACKNOWLEDGES THE JACK AND DORIS SMOTHERS ENDOWMENT IN TEXAS HISTORY, LIFE, AND CULTURE FOR ITS SUPPORT OF THIS PUBLICATION.

We dedicate this book to our families.
Thank you for believing in us!

Anyone can cook barbecue.
It is not as hard as people make it out to be.
It's just a really long day!

—JONNY WHITE

CONTENTS

BAR-B·Q

INTRODUCTION

"It's time to build a new fire," said the pitmaster as she handed an apprentice a shovel. It was the apprentice's first day at Goldee's Bar-B-Q, and even though she had no experience smoking meat and all that entailed, she was excited to learn. The pitmaster, who was a former apprentice herself, was glad to teach.

"Push these broken-down logs that are still burning to the back," said the pitmaster. "Then scoop out some of the ashes while leaving in the hot coals." The apprentice did what she was told while the pitmaster walked over to the log pile to grab more wood. When they returned, the pitmaster surveyed the apprentice's work and said it looked good. She then showed the apprentice what to do next.

The wind blew through the smokehouse, rattling sheets of foil and causing the flames to dance. It was a blustery morning in March, several hours before the restaurant would open at 11:00 a.m. Outside the smokehouse, a line of people had begun to form, with the first having arrived before dawn. Those waiting sat in camp chairs and on large coolers, some reading, some chatting, and others tossing a ball.

Inside the covered smokehouse, which was open-air with no door and walls made half with wood and half with window screens, were two sausage-shaped smokers that ran almost the entire length. These pits were refashioned from 1,000-gallon decommissioned propane tanks, a common housing for offset smokers in Texas. Outside the smokehouse was a smaller, 500-gallon version of the same.

A few months prior, Goldee's had been named the number-one barbecue restaurant in Texas by *Texas Monthly* magazine. Its young owners, who were also its pitmasters, were still adjusting to the increased volume that needed to be prepared to feed the long lines of hungry customers that came with this accolade.

Smoked meats, beans, slaw, potato salad, bread, pickles, and pudding were all on the menu, and while it was a jarring transition to go from cooking, say, ten briskets a day to cooking sixty, they were grateful for their good fortune.

Earlier, Lane, one of the owners, had asked the apprentice to add a log to the 500-gallon pit. He thought the wild wind was preventing it from coming up to temperature, and it needed an extra boost of fuel. The apprentice grabbed the fattest, largest log she could find on the pile.

She placed it on top of three logs that were already burning and then waited. And waited. And waited. Nothing happened. The log would not light, and it appeared that its heft was damping out the fire already blazing. "Maybe next time you could get a smaller log," offered Lane. The apprentice agreed and then the log caught. The fire would continue to burn.

Fire management was not the expected lesson that morning, but in barbecue, without fire you can't have smoke. Fire is at the heart of how we prepare our food at Goldee's. Of course, besides fire and smoke, there are other key steps to creating our barbecue, such as gathering our tools and choosing our meats. Once we have our meats, we are very particular about how we trim and season each piece.

After our meats are ready to cook, we then place them on the smoker, build our fires, control the temperature, and assess the meat's progress as it transforms. Finally, we use our judgment about when it's ready, then wrap it and let it rest before serving. We take all these steps for each cook, and you can't forgo any. They all work together.

Besides smoked meats, we also have our sides to prepare, as well as our sauces, pickles, desserts, and bread. Every single item on the tray we serve at Goldee's has been made by hand. We want that slice of bread to be as good as that juicy rib. No detail escapes our attention.

At Goldee's, we understand the nature of teamwork and how each element plays a vital part. Our staff is a tight crew, and each member helps bring our food to your table. Barbecue is a group effort. Of course, you at home may be cooking everything alone, but if you have someone to help you, the work flows much more easily. At Goldee's, there is no single pitmaster, no single person making the sides, no single person baking our bread. Instead, our small team pulls together and we all play a role in creating this meal.

If you're holding this book, then most likely you want to learn how to cook barbecue. Thank you for placing your trust in us. Whether you've been smoking meats all your life or it's your first day learning the craft, we are here to show you the way.

Now, people like to go on about discovering pitmasters' secrets, but here's our biggest secret—we have no secrets. That's right. We want everyone to be able to make good barbecue, so why not share all that we know? Yes, we may have been named number one, but we are in competition only with ourselves. We work every day to improve our skills, and we hope that by sharing our knowledge we can enable you to make good barbecue too.

This cookbook celebrates our blend of classic Texas barbecue with new-wave ideas and techniques. Our aim, in both our restaurant and our book, is to honor classic Texan barbecue techniques while also working toward a future where the best barbecue is available to all.

We achieve this by embracing our diversity, opening doors for anyone who wishes to enter, and constantly innovating our methods. We also challenge everyone, including ourselves, to do their best. And if we fail, we simply try to do better the next time.

This cookbook showcases our hallmark recipes from the pit room, which include smoked meats such as brisket, pork ribs, beef ribs, sausage, and turkey. It also includes the side dishes that come from our kitchen, such as our sauces, potato salad, cheesy grits, coleslaw, and beans. We also reveal the multiday process behind our homemade bread,

the surprise contained in our banana pudding, and our method for a Laotian-Texan smoked beef sausage.

Because smoking meats is at the heart of what we do, we provide plenty of details about how we cook each protein, following a ten-step method that mirrors how we work at the restaurant.

We give this entire process the shortened name *the cook*, a term we use throughout this book. When we refer to the cook, we're talking about the process, not the person actually cooking, which in the barbecue world is known as a pit hand or pitmaster.

While there are standard approaches to Texas barbecue that have been presented before, we do a few things differently. Here, we share all of our techniques so anyone can replicate our number-one barbecue in their backyard.

Through stories, photos, and recipes, we invite anyone who wishes to improve their barbecue game into our smokehouse and kitchen. We want you to experience what it's like to work with us as an apprentice and learn firsthand how to cook like we do. And as you read along and learn to improve your own barbecue with this crew, we won't even ask you to sweep the pit room!

We feel that the world is a much better place with beautiful barbecue. We already have three former apprentices who have opened their own restaurants, and we couldn't be happier. We learned so much from our prior barbecue jobs, and being able to pass on that wisdom and see it catch fire with others is a true reward.

If you are willing to learn, we are here to teach. We have nothing to hide. Barbecue isn't a difficult craft, but it does take patience. If you follow our guidelines and invest the hours, you will create a beautiful tray of food for your family and friends.

Don't worry—it's not all work here at Goldee's. We fully embrace the slow pace of smoking meats, so there's downtime too. That's why you'll sometimes find us playing video games, frying doughnuts, or swinging a log at a ball made of foil in a pickup game of baseball in the parking lot. The meat needs time, but with patience you'll be well on your way to beautiful barbecue.

We apply this balanced philosophy at the restaurant, and we also teach this to our apprentices. Most of us began cooking barbecue later in life, and from our experiences we've learned what works and what doesn't. Using our collective knowledge from our time at some of the top barbecue restaurants in the state of Texas, we forged our own path.

If you open a barbecue book or go on YouTube, you'll see lots of rules, often shared with the caveat that if you deviate from the rules, your barbecue will fail. We think this is crazy. Sure, there are steps we always follow. But we're also flexible. In barbecue, there are far too many variables outside of your control. If you are attached to following a path set in stone, you will be disappointed. Fire doesn't work like that.

Instead, we teach our apprentices what we can control, such as how to trim meat, season meat, build fires, aim for the right temperatures, and know when to pull and wrap the meat.

There will be multiple variables along the way, however, such as wind, the shape of the meat, the humidity, and things that we can't even articulate because what happens to a piece of meat in the cooker is an alchemy that we can only guide; ultimately, it is out of our control. The only way to become good at cooking is to become one with the entire process and follow your instincts.

For instance, take a brisket. The popular view is that you need to pull it from the smoker at a temperature of 205°F. You'll see people cooking their briskets with a temperature probe stuck into it, and when an alarm goes off saying it's hit the target temp, they'll pull it, wrap it, let it rest, and then cut into it.

Now, maybe it was ready to go, but maybe it wasn't. See, the temperature of the brisket varies by how often you've opened the smoking chamber's door, how many other pieces of meat were cooking beside it, and other factors. Its temperature is only one of many factors to consider when deciding whether your brisket is done.

We consider the texture and color of the meat's surface, how the meat feels when probed with something sharp, and the flexibility of the piece as we hold it in our hands. Sometimes the temperature is nowhere close to what the rule makers say it should be, but if all the other factors tell us it's time, then we'll pull it anyway.

This is the main thing we try to convey to our apprentices—how to go with the flow and cook with your instincts. No two cooks will ever be the same. If you're following a strict set of rules, then yeah, this may freak you out. You may start worrying about dirty smoke or not keeping the pit to an exact temperature or whatnot.

This is nonsense. Barbecue is meant to be fun! If you're equipped with a solid framework of knowledge, and you can embrace the freedom to work within this structure, we know that you will be a better cook. Not only will you be able to make your own delicious smoked meats, but—even better—you also will learn to create your own style of barbecue.

We aim to teach and share what we've learned. We're not gatekeepers and we've held nothing back. There are no secrets in barbecue. We are just doing our best. And we are here to help you do your best so you can light a fire and build your own barbecue dream.

1 THE GOLDEE'S ST

ORY

Our founders (left to right): Nupohn Inthanousay, Jonny White, Jalen Heard, Lane M[illegible] and Dylan Taylor

Before we tell you our story, which isn't all that remarkable, just know that what makes us special is that we all like each other and enjoy working together as a team. Maybe it comes from our years playing music together in bands, or maybe it comes from our years of living together in one house, but we've figured out how to combine work and play in a harmonious environment. We know that we are stronger together than apart.

Now, we might have some specific experiences that may or may not inspire your own barbecue journey, but what makes Goldee's a success and our barbecue taste good is that we all have the same goal—a tray of barbecue that's better than the one we made the day before. That's it.

We're not afraid to challenge each other, and we may occasionally get on each other's nerves. At the same time, we enjoy hanging out together and think it's really cool that we have built this life doing what we love.

Before we continue, let us introduce ourselves. There are five owners—Jalen Heard, Lane Milne, Jonny White, Dylan Taylor, and Nupohn Inthanousay. While these days it's only Lane, Jalen, Jonny, and Nupohn who are still working at the restaurant, in the beginning it was all of us.

Our barbecue story begins in kindergarten at the appropriately named Wood Elementary in Arlington, Texas. It was here that Jalen and Lane became friends. Dylan joined them in third grade, and in fourth grade, Jonny moved from Georgia to Texas and fell in with the crew. Nupohn arrived in the area in junior high, and by the time we were in ninth grade at Arlington's Martin High School, we were a tightly bound pack.

During these years, we started playing music and formed a band. Jonny sang and played drums, Lane and Dylan played guitar, Nupohn was on keys, and Jalen had the car. When we graduated, we decided to continue the music while also going to school. It took a while, but after a year, we were all in Austin, the Live Music Capital of the World.

Dylan and Lane arrived in Austin first, attending classes down the road at Texas State University in San Marcos. One cold, rainy day, they decided to skip class and go get barbecue at Franklin Barbecue. If for some reason you're not familiar with Franklin, it's run by a guy named Aaron Franklin and it's been lauded as one of the best barbecue restaurants in the world. He's gotten heaps of praise, and his crazy long lines reflect that.

Usually, you'll spend hours waiting for his food. But if it's cold and rainy, you might have a chance of getting in with a much shorter wait. That day, Lane and Dylan drove by Franklin to see how the line was and yep, it was short.

They joined the queue, made it to the counter, ordered a tray, and then sat down and took their first bite. The brisket was smoky, juicy, and peppery, and it was unlike anything they had eaten before. There was nothing wrong with the barbecue they grew up with in Arlington, but this barbecue was on another level.

After that trip to Franklin, Dylan and Lane started going to lunch in between classes, becoming regulars at local spots such as La Barbecue and Micklethwait Craft Meats. As Lane says, they realized that not only could barbecue be made by young guys like us, but it also could be made with care and precision. Barbecue could be cool.

At Micklethwait, for instance, there was homemade bread and lemon juice and poppy seeds in the coleslaw. This was a far cry from the slices of commodity white bread and gloopy coleslaw that came from a tub that we'd eaten back home.

After that first year, Jalen, Jonny, and Nupohn joined the crew in Austin. One April day, we headed out to Lockhart to take Nupohn skydiving for his birthday. Lockhart is a small Texas town that's about half an hour away from Austin. It's home to three legendary old-school barbecue restaurants—Kreuz Market, Smitty's, and Black's—which have been open for decades. Because these restaurants are so revered, the Texas legislature has named Lockhart the Barbecue Capital of Texas.

That day, we ate at Black's. It was satisfying, but we also noticed the differences between it and the new-school barbecue we'd been eating in Austin. You could say it was more primal, with a focus on the meat.

The older Texas spots, which include Louie Mueller Barbecue in Taylor and City Market in Luling, two other small Central Texas towns also about half an hour away from Austin, began as meat markets. The barbecue came about because they needed a way to sell the meats that hadn't been bought fresh. Smoking them helped them last longer and prevented waste. Originally, there were no sides and no sauces available, just meat and perhaps a sleeve of saltines.

This is where you get the Central Texas tradition of serving barbecue with butcher paper, because that's how these markets originally offered their meats. It wasn't until recently that these spots sold accompaniments on the side. Even when they conceded to demand, they kept their offerings slim, sticking to the classic barbecue side-dish trinity of potato salad, coleslaw, and pinto beans.

Despite this simplicity, these restaurants were still very good. The buildings were often encased in a black patina from years of smoke, and the old pits, sometimes fueled by an open fire on the ground, had been cooking meats for decades. You could feel the history. Like the spots in Austin, these small-town restaurants were producing a style of barbecue unlike anything we'd grown up with in North Texas.

After our first trip to Lockhart, we started balancing our barbecue excursions between these old spots and the new. We all became obsessed. Soon after, Dylan dropped out of college so he could work full-time at a barbecue restaurant. He wanted to know everything.

He began in the pit room at the newly opened Terry Black's, which was run by young twins Mark and Mike Black. (If that name sounds familiar, they are related to the same Black family of Lockhart barbecue fame, though the two sides have separate businesses.)

Anyway, we all started visiting Dylan at his new job and became good friends with Mark and Mike. They were super generous in sharing with us all they had learned growing up in one of the state's oldest barbecue families. It was inspiring. And in the following months, one by one, the rest of us quit school (except for Jonny, who, in hindsight, had been wise not to even enroll) and began to take shifts at different barbecue places around town.

Lane worked at Freedmen's, then Micklethwait; Jalen also worked at Freedmen's, then moved to Banger's; Dylan started at Terry Black's, then was at La Barbecue and Truth Barbecue in Brenham; and Jonny spent time at Valentina's, La Barbecue, and Franklin. Nupohn wasn't working in barbecue but was getting valuable front-of-the-house experience at a Thai place, where he was the general manager.

When we weren't at our restaurant jobs, on our days off we'd cook barbecue in the backyard of the East Austin house we shared. At first, we had only a grill that Nupohn's family gave us, which Dylan warped when he placed large logs onto it, not knowing that the thin metal wouldn't be able to withstand the heat. (This is a common rookie mistake, so if you've also made it, know that you're not alone.)

Next, we had Lane's dad's old pit, which was a step up, as it was an offset smoker. In an offset smoker the firebox sits apart from the cooking chamber. At the other end of the cooker, there's a smokestack, which pulls the heat and smoke from the box, through the cooker, and out of the pit. This style is what most Central Texas pitmasters use, both old-school and new.

This old pit didn't warp, thankfully. Though it had been in Lane's family for over thirty years and it had issues like the firebox falling off, we still made it work. In between our trips to various barbecue spots to learn and taste everything on offer, we began to develop our smoked-meat palate. We cooked hundreds of briskets, ribs, and turkeys during this time, and yeah, most were terrible, but we were having a blast learning new techniques.

Dylan decided to step up our cooking game, and after he began working as a welder at Austin Smoke Works, he fabricated a 500-gallon smoker. We decided to host a pop-up at Fleet Coffee, which was our favorite place to get caffeinated in East Austin, and we wanted to use his new smoker for our event.

The only problem was that we needed to move it from the workshop to our house. None of us had ever towed anything before, but Jonny volunteered to do the job. We were all worried, though, about pulling such a heavy, awkward item through Austin. And wouldn't you know it but the day Jonny was supposed to bring it to our house, it was rainy and slippery.

After a stressful trip, he did manage to get it to our house with no mishaps. But there was another problem—we couldn't figure out how to move it into the backyard. Until we came up with a solution, we had to park it on a side street. After assuring our neighbors it wouldn't be out there forever, we still worried that someone would come along and steal it. Fortunately, this didn't happen, and after a week or so, we managed to squeeze it into the yard.

Now, at this time, we were proud of our cooking. It takes a lot of confidence to put on a barbecue pop-up, and as five young guys, we had plenty of that! In retrospect, though, what we made just wasn't all that good. If you ask friends who attended these first gatherings, they'll most likely be diplomatic and say, "Well, perhaps there was room for improvement. But hey, we still had fun!"

Fun is a vital factor in barbecue, and we were glad we could provide a relaxing and inviting atmosphere for our backyard guests. But we were also keen to hone our barbecue skills, so we kept cooking. Since then, our tray has evolved quite a bit, and we're thankful that our friends never gave up on us. Of course, they still tease us about the old days, which is fine. It reminds us how much we've grown.

For instance, the original beans we served were sweet baked beans. If you've had our beans now, you know that they're meaty chili beans, but we started by making beans with lots of sugar, ketchup, and mustard. Lane can trace each step of development from those sweet beans to our savory beans, but most of us can't see any similarities between the two, which is a good thing since those baked beans weren't very good.

Anyway, we kept working shifts at barbecue joints and testing recipes on our days off from work. Eventually, it all started coming together. By 2019, we decided it was time to open our own spot. We felt Austin didn't need another barbecue restaurant, so we headed home to North Texas, where all our families still lived.

Goldee's, before the crowd arrives.

When we first set our sights on DFW (as we refer to the Dallas–Fort Worth metro area), we had friends with a building in the lively Deep Ellum neighborhood in Dallas. This area, close to downtown, has a history rooted in a variety of cultures, including African American, Mexican, Czech, and Jewish. This mosaic of influences has given Deep Ellum a vibrant musical and culinary tradition, but this spot was going to cost way too much money.

Next, we considered a spot in Arlington, which sits in between Dallas and Fort Worth. It's not only where we grew up but also where both the Dallas Cowboys and Texas Rangers sports teams play their home games. There's also a major university, University of Texas at Arlington. This spot was close to both the stadiums and the school, and it received lots of foot traffic.

Again, the rent would have been over our budget, and the last thing we wanted was to take on outside investors. To help raise the money for our restaurant, we'd been teaching classes, and we had about $60,000 in the bank. That was our target, and we didn't want to stray too far from it and get into debt.

We kept looking, but nothing seemed to fit. We were discouraged. One day, however, Lane's mom was driving down Dick Price Road, the main thoroughfare of Kennedale, Texas, a rural stretch between Arlington and Fort Worth. There's not much there besides a landfill, a used-car lot, pastures, and the occasional homestead. But people need to eat, and there was also an old restaurant in that mix that had a "For Rent" sign in the window.

She let us know about the building, and we went to take a look. Even though it was close to most of the action of Fort Worth, driving that last country mile to the restaurant, you'd swear you were in the middle of nowhere. This isolation worked to our advantage, as the rent was incredibly cheap.

The space was perfect for our needs, as it was already pretty much up to code. It had a working commercial kitchen with grease traps, vent hoods, and all that stuff, along with key kitchen equipment like a stove and ovens. It was a cool spot and needed only a bit of cosmetic work. And did we mention that it was dirt cheap?

Besides being affordable, what was even more cool was that it had once been a barbecue spot called Kenneth's Pit Barbecue. It opened in the early 1970s and operated for almost thirty years. While we were remodeling the building, people would stop and tell us their memories of eating at Kenneth's. Heck, even Lane's family had been customers back in the day.

After Kenneth retired and closed the restaurant, a taqueria moved into the space. It didn't last very long, though, and when we took over, the locals were thrilled to have it be a barbecue restaurant once again.

As we took down the previous restaurant's signage, on the metal frame we saw an outline of the letters from when it had been a barbecue spot. Using that as a guide, Dylan harnessed himself to the top and repainted the most important element, which read "BAR-B-Q."

He filled in the large letters by hand with black paint, and while it may look rough to some, it gets the message across. It may not be fancy, but you can tell it was crafted by hand, just like our food.

Now if you squint at the sign during the day, you can also see the faded text from its time with Kenneth, such as his hours and services offered. Another interesting artifact of the building's past is a brick rotisserie smoker that's wedged into the corner of our smokehouse and the kitchen. It's no longer operational (though some old customers insist that it could be), but it brings a historical flair to the restaurant.

We did the remodeling ourselves, learning from Google tutorials and YouTube videos as we went along. Jonny's grandpa helped us build the smokehouse for our two 10,000-gallon Mill Scale pits. For that, we poured a cement slab, erected walls and a roof, and wired up some lights.

We placed the smokehouse perpendicular to the restaurant with the flow of the line in mind. When people arrive, they are right outside the smokehouse. Since it's open with screened-in windows, the customers can see us cooking and ask us questions. The roof juts out, forming an awning, which provides shade and shelter for people while they wait.

When the customers finally enter the restaurant, we greet them with a sample of meat, ask where they're from, and then take their order. The cutter slices and stacks their meats, another grabs the sides, and the customers pay and then take a seat in the dining room. At the other end of the dining room is the exit. The whole process from waiting to leaving is a smooth course. It flows.

We know a lot about flow from working with our smokers (more on that later), and we wanted our dining experience to have the same easy, chill movement. We spent a lot of time contemplating our dining experience since we had waited in plenty of lines ourselves. Our philosophy was that we wanted our customers to be treated as we wanted to be treated ourselves. This is the Goldee's rule.

After we painted the exterior of our building red, we had an Austin artist friend, Peelander-Yellow, come and paint a mural on the front. He had created a wall painting on our house in East Austin, and we loved his vibrant, cheerful style, which had the energy of old-school New York Street artists like Keith Haring.

For our restaurant, he came up with a yellow cow who's holding a fork and gazing at a sausage speared on the tines. Inside the cow, our name is spelled out in rounded, bouncy letters that are light blue, orange, and red. It's unlike anything we'd seen in Texas barbecue before, and we felt that this street-style graphic paired with the more traditional shack-like building captured our vibe of old meets new.

When we were trying to come up with our restaurant's name, we spent a year going back and forth on different options. At one point, we had a list with over a hundred choices, including Dumpy's, Red House, and Price's, among others. We had a hard time reaching an agreement, and at one point, most of us felt Secondhand Smokehouse was the best choice. Still, Jonny didn't love it, and the rest of us wondered if we were making a mistake.

Back when we had lived in Austin, Dylan owned an old Ford truck he'd use to haul his smoker to catering gigs and classes. The truck was painted bright gold, which inspired

MILL SCALE
METAL WORKS
LOCKHART, TX
FOX
BROS

his girlfriend to affectionately name the truck Goldie. This truck had been a key player in helping us raise the funds we needed to open the restaurant. Goldie the truck was a valued early member of our team.

Time passed, and we were growing frustrated with our inability to decide on the name. None of them felt quite right. One day Dylan was discussing his beloved truck, then he paused and said, "Why don't we just call the restaurant Goldie?" Of course! We all agreed that this was the one. It was short, sweet, and memorable. It also celebrated an important time in our history.

As for the spelling, when we were working with our logo designer, he suggested that we end it with a double e, much like the popular Texas travel center Buc-ee's. He explained it would be more graphic, which would give it a stronger impact on signs, shirts, and other merchandise. We said heck yeah and made the change. Our name was now Goldee's.

When we were creating our menu, we wanted to dial in only the best dishes and not overload our menu with lots of superfluous items. To do this, we stuck with traditional Texas meats and sides such as brisket, pork ribs, sausage, beans, potato salad, and coleslaw. For dessert, we would have banana pudding.

As for testing our food, we strove to create our favorite of each item. After visiting so many barbecue spots, we had a firm idea of what we liked and didn't like. We used that as a guide, along with our vision to create balanced tastes that could appeal to everyone.

For instance, take our potato salad. In Texas, you'll typically see two styles—a mustard-based potato salad that's bright yellow and super tangy, or a mayonnaise-based potato salad that's white and skews more sweet. A customer can look at the potato salad and instantly know what style it is, and if it's not their preference, then they probably won't order it.

If, however, you combine the two styles into one, you can create a dish that's hard to label yet will still hit all the right notes. Even better, if you just call it "potato salad," without any other description, then most likely the customer will try it, at least once. This is what we did. And because we created a balanced potato salad that's our favorite, we believe it may become your favorite too.

After three months of remodeling and menu development, it was now May 2019 and we were ready to open our doors. There was only one problem. Even though our renovations had been mainly cosmetic, because we'd increased the occupancy by bringing in longer tables and creating outdoor space, our septic system didn't pass the county's muster. It was too small, and we'd need to get a larger tank.

No problem, we thought, and we got right on it. One hurdle led to another, and trying to solve this one issue prevented us from opening for another nine months. We had our space, we had our name, we had our logo, and we had our menu. We were ready to open, but the county inspector had different ideas.

Instead of opening, we waited. And waited. Who knew that one septic tank could derail our plans and cause so many problems? Oh well, it is what it is. During our downtime, we decided to keep fine-tuning our menu. Dylan taught classes, and we had a few pop-ups, two in Atlanta with our friends at Fox Bros. Bar-B-Q and others at Zavala Barbecue in nearby Grand Prairie, Texas. All were well received and sold out. We kept busy, but we were also eager to solve our septic woes so we could begin service in our own space.

Finally we passed the inspection, and two weeks later we had our grand opening. Our first service was on Saturday, February 15, 2020. People started arriving early in the morning and by ten o'clock, the line snaked around the entire parking lot and began to head out onto the road.

That first day, we did fifty briskets, twenty-nine racks of ribs, sixteen turkeys, and lots of sausages. We sold out in three hours. There wasn't enough parking, and it was chaotic in the lot. But other than that, everything went well and people kept telling us just how much they loved our food. It was such an amazing day. The next three weekends we were open Friday, Saturday, and Sunday, and it was steady and good. Then, COVID-19 hit. We shut down the dining room after only thirteen services.

A typical morning before service at Goldee's.

ADT

For a month, we were trying to figure out what our game plan would be. For the first five weeks, we vacuum-sealed our meats and sold everything to go. Then we began doing curbside with our full menu, serving it in to-go packaging. Some customers would then open it while it was still warm and eat it in their car or on their hood. Others took it home. We continued operating that way for almost a year.

Despite these hardships, we began to attract some regulars. For instance, there's a man named Joe who stopped by every weekend. He'd also come to visit us while we were cooking late at night, and he became one of our biggest advocates, bringing family and friends with him as he helped spread the word.

Because our opening had been heralded by the press, we had food writers stop by as well. The first major article came from Sarah Blaskovich of the *Dallas Morning News*. We didn't recognize her, but she introduced herself and asked lots of questions. Even though we accidentally got her order wrong (we served her the wrong sausage), she didn't seem to notice, and we didn't freak out too much after we realized our error. Her article declared Goldee's the best barbecue in DFW. We were over the moon.

One cloudy winter day, a familiar face pulled up in a dark German sedan. The driver was a confident man with horn-rimmed glasses, a gimme cap advertising an Austin barbecue spot, and a T-shirt featuring another. It was Daniel Vaughn, the barbecue editor of *Texas Monthly*, who was also known as the BBQ Snob. His opinions and influence had the power to change lives.

The first time we ran into Daniel, it wasn't at Goldee's. Instead, it was during our downtime before opening. Lane and Jonny had decided to visit Cattleack Barbecue in Farmer's Branch, Texas. Cattleack is a two-time *Texas Monthly* top-ten barbecue restaurant, and we were excited to finally try it. It's only open on Thursdays and Fridays along with one Saturday a month. This scarcity creates long lines, and the day Jonny and Lane visited, there were lots of people waiting, true to form.

That day, Daniel Vaughn was standing in front of them in line. He had no idea who they were, and Lane and Jonny didn't say anything, but they knew exactly who he was. As soon as they reached the counter to order, Daniel turned around and offered to let them cut ahead of him since his dining companion hadn't arrived yet. They thanked him, had an incredible meal, and that was the end of their exchange.

When Daniel finally made it to Goldee's, he took his to-go order and ate it right there in his car. We were all freaking out to have him there. Fortunately, even though it was still curbside, he raved about everything, especially the ribs. *Texas Monthly* soon sent a photographer to take our picture for a feature about how barbecue restaurants were faring during COVID. This was major validation for us.

At the beginning of 2021, it had been two years since we'd begun our time on Dick Price Road and almost a year of doing curbside service only. We were tired. Dylan left Texas to work on a ranch in Colorado, and Jonny went to Egypt to consult on a Texas barbecue concept in Cairo. The three who remained, Lane, Jalen, and Nupohn, were able to keep the business running since it was still extremely slow. To help when needed, Nupohn's little brother PJ also joined the team.

When Jonny returned to Kennedale, we decided to open the dining room again, and through the spring and summer business was steady but not anything close to our opening day. Making ends meet was a challenge, and we contemplated selling one of our 1,000-gallon pits to raise some cash.

Every four years, *Texas Monthly* magazine publishes a ranking of the top fifty barbecue spots in the state. All the pitmasters had worked for restaurants that had landed in the top ten, and we were well aware of the list's ability to change lives. Daniel Vaughn spearheads the effort, but the entire magazine is involved with the judging. We hadn't seen Daniel at Goldee's in a while and had no idea whether other magazine staffers had visited or not.

Fortunately, we believe that every customer should be treated the same, so it didn't matter who came through the line—each was equally important. We'd seen pitmasters trot out a hidden stash of superior meats when Daniel or another food writer visited, and this didn't sit well with us. We wanted everyone to receive the best we had to offer.

On Friday, October 15, 2021, we were in a meeting after service ended when Jonny received a text. It was the cover of the "50 Best BBQ Joints" issue of *Texas Monthly*. The image was a stylized photograph of our tray. It took us a moment, but we realized that if we were on the cover, then we must be number one. Holy shit!

Now, before we began getting too crazy, we recognized that we had a problem. See, this photo was a leak, and the official announcement wouldn't be made until Monday. As much as we wanted to shout out to the entire world that we were the best in Texas, we realized it was wiser to keep quiet. Who knows? Maybe there were even multiple covers and we didn't land the top slot. We had to wait until *Texas Monthly* made its announcement.

The next few days were rough. And yes, after a fitful weekend of little sleep, a rib class in Lockhart for Jonny, cases of White Claw, and rounds of Fortnite, we finally received the confirmation on Monday morning that after being open for only a year and a half, we were now the new top spot for barbecue in Texas.

We spent the day drinking champagne down the road at Zavala's with other barbecue friends who had also made the list. Then we returned to the restaurant to prepare for what was next. If history was any prediction, we would be busy. We placed an order for more wood and meat.

NO
MEANIES

THE GOLDEE'S WAY, OUR CORE VALUES

When you walk into Goldee's, you'll see a sign by the cutting board that says, "No Meanies." Today, the sign is a hand painting of the phrase with a dachshund. But from the beginning, we've written "no meanies" on our menu boards and various signs scribbled onto butcher paper and posted by the block.

You'll hear customers comment on it, usually with a chuckle. But it's not there to be funny. Sure, the cute dog and the phrasing are light, but we do not tolerate people being cruel—to us or the other customers.

We don't care where you came from, what you believe, or with whom you consort—everyone is welcome at our table. If you are disparaging to another in our restaurant, you need to leave. This behavior is *not* welcome.

When the *New York Times* profiled new and upcoming Texas barbecue restaurants in the summer of 2023, we were included along with Barbs-B-Q, a new Lockhart spot that one of our former apprentices and pitmasters, Chuck Charnichart, had recently opened. The article mentioned that Barbs was following the Goldee's template, which got us thinking.

We had never formally written down any template or list of what we believe. However, we could see that there were certain values we pass on to our employees.

Goldee's doesn't stand just for excellent food. It's a way of being. Give your best to the world and it will be returned to you. Sure, we're only human and sometimes we falter. For the most part, though, we do our best to incorporate these principles into our daily work. It has not only helped us cook amazing barbecue but also created a welcoming place to both work and eat.

NO MEANIES: Be kind, inclusive, and welcoming to all.

EMBRACE YOUR ROOTS: Give back to your community and appreciate those who came before you.

BE INQUISITIVE: Ask questions and learn to define what you enjoy.

BE CURIOUS: Eat everything, and travel far and wide to experience new tastes.

KEEP GROWING: Strive to be better. Each cook is unique, so think about how you can improve. What would you do differently this time?

PATIENCE: Go with the flow and enjoy yourself as your barbecue journey unfolds. Barbecue takes time.

IMMERSE YOURSELF: Learn all aspects of the business and know that no one is above doing anything. We are a team; we are one.

BALANCE: Work is more fun with recreation. Incorporate play into your day.

BE GENEROUS: There are no secrets and there's nothing to hide. A generous spirit lives forever. Give back and share.

FOLLOW YOUR HEART: Love what you create.

2 THE STAGES OF C

OOKING BARBECUE

Before we go further into *how* we cook, let's discuss *what* we're cooking. At Goldee's, we are cooking barbecue, which is meat cooked with fire and smoke. We're not going to dive into the history of barbecue—we'll leave that to the experts. Just know that Texas is so vast that within the state there are four distinct barbecue styles, which include Central Texas, East Texas, South Texas, and West Texas (see sidebar). We're cooking our interpretation of the Central Texas style.

For those who aren't familiar, Central Texas barbecue is probably what most people think of when they consider Texas smoked meats. As the name implies, it is rooted in the central part of the state, and it is cooked in offset smokers. In an offset smoker, the cooking chamber is separate from the fire chamber. This style of cooking is also known as indirect heat. (For comparison, when you cook steaks on a grill with the fire underneath the meat, this is direct heat.)

For seasoning, the Central Texas style keeps it simple with salt, pepper, and occasionally seasoning salt. The assumption that salt and pepper are the only seasonings allowed is simply not true anymore. Many barbecue restaurants have long used seasoning salts for extra oomph, including one of the oldest in the state, Smitty's Market in Lockhart.

Beef is king in Central Texas barbecue, with slices of tender, juicy brisket being its flagship offering. The Texas trinity is brisket, sausage, and pork ribs, and barbecue pilgrims will typically judge a restaurant by the quality of these three offerings.

The Central Texas style evolved from the meat markets found in small towns close to Austin such as Lockhart, Taylor, and Luling. These markets were often run by German, Czech, and other Eastern European immigrants to Texas, and they would preserve older cuts by smoking them. Trimmings were crafted into sausage.

Because these were markets and not sit-down restaurants, the meat was served to customers wrapped in red butcher paper. While side dishes were not sold, you could usually get pickles, raw white onion slices, crackers, white bread, and maybe a wedge of cheddar cheese to go with the meat.

Sauces were initially considered an insult in the late 1800s and early 1900s, since they often were used to mask inferior meats. To serve the meat with a sauce would have been an admission that perhaps the meat wasn't the highest quality.

Times change, however, and as the style evolved, sauces began appearing because of demand from customers. Side dishes also became part of the cannon. The three most common accompaniments to smoked meats are potato salad, coleslaw, and pinto beans. The potato salad and coleslaw have Eastern European roots, and their tangy, cool, and crisp qualities are a good foil to the rich, smoky meats.

Pinto beans are a decidedly Texas addition, as the bean is native to the Southwest region and has long been a favorite of Texans from all walks of life. These pintos are typically cooked in a savory style with onions, garlic, jalapeños, chili powder, and sometimes even smoked meats.

We don't see saltines and cheese wedges offered too often these days, though they were more common in the earlier days of Texas barbecue. However, white bread, pickles, and raw onions are still standard additions to each barbecue tray. The use of sauce is still heavily disputed, and while it's always offered, it will be on the side. Apply sauce at your own discretion, but we always recommend trying the meat without it first.

For dessert, banana pudding has become the most popular way to conclude your barbecue meal. If you look at early Texas pudding recipes, you'll see that it was once a layered trifle made with custard, vanilla wafers, and a meringue. The meringue has disappeared these days, but the custard and cookies remain.

These historically significant items were our inspiration for our restaurant's menu. We wanted to pay homage to the classic Central Texas tray. We cook our meats in offset smokers; we offer the trinity of brisket, sausage, and ribs. Our sides include potato salad, coleslaw, and pinto beans. And we offer homemade pickles, sauce, and bread.

We've also added a few twists on our menu to reflect the diversity of our own backgrounds, such as our Laotian sausage, which adds Southeast Asian flavorings to a classic Texas beef link. As we develop new recipes, we always keep our Central Texas background firmly in mind and tailor those techniques to each new protein and accompaniment.

Some might say that our style is also known as "craft barbecue." This is a term that came about in the early 2010s, and it reflects the trend of pitmasters using higher quality meats, not skimping on the preparation of side dishes, and using all wood to power their smokers. Nothing electric, nothing premade, and nothing fast. Craft barbecue takes time, patience, and consistency to get right.

It can be a challenge to produce craft barbecue on a large scale, as we do. In terms of rankings and such, it's this commitment that elevates us from one spot to another. Craft barbecue spots are open only for limited hours and days, and long lines and "sold out" signs can be common if the spot becomes popular. Because of the attention to detail, when the food is gone, it can't easily be replenished. It has already taken several days to prepare.

However, the good news for home cooks is that it's a heck of a lot easier to dial in your barbecue skills when you are focused on smoking smaller batches. It's easier to trim one brisket than 150. It's easier to season two racks of ribs than 240. It's easier to stuff 5 pounds of sausage versus 500. You get the idea.

Yet we've been consistently producing for our customers a tray that's rooted in this from-scratch approach. Craft barbecue doesn't feel homogenized or mass produced. We're glad to share what we've learned so you can easily re-create our style at home.

Now, people often ask, "What is your secret?" We've had hundreds come through our doors to learn from us, people who come from a variety of viewpoints, whether it's restaurateurs looking to add a smoked meat program to their menus, longtime pitmasters wishing to learn new skills, or home cooks who are focused on feeding their loved ones rather than a crowd.

While we all worked in a variety of restaurants, at heart, we're backyard guys. When you're cooking in a backyard, you have the advantage of concentration. After our shifts at our respective jobs at joints around Austin, we'd come home, fire up our smoker, and collectively apply what we'd learned and then transform that into a formula that could work for that particular cook.

In barbecue, *a cook* is the shorthand term for your time cooking the meat on the smoker. It does not refer to the person who's preparing the meat. Sure, you could call them a cook, though you can also call them a pitmaster or a pit hand. It's just a label, but use of the term *cook* to refer to the process is common across all platforms, whether you're cooking in a restaurant or in your yard. Each session on the smoker is a cook.

In this book, we will use that phrase often. Many people like to keep journals of each cook, jotting down the number of fires built, where the meat was positioned, how the meat changed as it was bathed in smoke and heat, and the final assessment—how the meat tasted.

Consistency is the hallmark of a top-tier barbecue restaurant, and the easiest way to dial this in is to not cook too much. Scale in barbecue is challenging, and to reach the highest levels of quality with such large quantities is tough. You would need a large space filled with multiple pits, an extensive team, and plenty of funds to keep this large operation going, and even then, it's not easy to produce top-tier meats. Usually, something has to give.

The good news, if you're a home cook, is that the principles of craft barbecue are easily within reach. You're probably only cooking a brisket or two, a couple racks of ribs, and perhaps a turkey. If you're interested in making sausage, it's far easier to dial in your technique when working with 4 pounds of meat instead of 100.

We believe some of the best smoked meats come out of small, backyard pits. Now, we cook for a small crowd every weekend, yet with our small team we've been able to create a tray that meets our backyard standards. People ask why we're not open all week or for dinner, and it's for this reason alone. We want our restaurant to have that intimacy you get from a gathering with friends and family.

Working in restaurants, we had some bosses that gave us their instructions and told us not to deviate from the list. Every step in the cook had to follow explicit directions. For backyard guys used to tinkering, this was frustrating. We knew that no cook is ever the same since there are far too many variables that can affect how it goes. Having to stay in one lane when sometimes a small veer to the left or right would get you better results is limiting.

Instead, when we opened our own place, we knew that there would be certain elements that could easily remain the same, such as how the meat was trimmed, how it was seasoned, how it was placed on the smoker, and our target temperature as we cooked.

But we also had enough insight into the process to be flexible. Is the wind blowing extra hard? Then maybe we'll keep the firebox door closed so the flames don't die. Is the meat cooking too fast? Then perhaps we'll build lower fires and shift it away from the firebox exchange into the smoker.

As this point, perhaps some of the words being written here are still gibberish to you. That's okay. Keep reading. Barbecue is a multilayered process that takes time to understand. Persistence is what leads to mastery.

The one thing that we want to stress, however, is that no two cooks are ever the same, even if you're following a concisely outlined cooking method. The key is to understand that there are plenty of variables and if you're flexible, you'll not only become more fluent in cooking smoked meats but also begin to develop your own techniques. Our words are merely a guide.

We reckon that the secret to our consistency and quality is that we know our limits, we are flexible with what we do, and, while some things demand precision, there is still plenty of room to experiment and see what happens.

We spend our days working toward our services on Friday, Saturday, and Sunday. People are surprised if we sell out of food, but because each meal takes multiple days to prepare, when it's gone, it's gone.

At home, you most likely won't be aiming to feed hundreds at one time (though if you are, we salute your ambition!), so you probably won't need seven days to cook for each gathering. But the steps to reach the end will be the same, and this is what we're going to walk you through as you smoke each meat and cook each side.

While we could simply give you a time frame and temperature for the smoked meats, we feel it's important to outline every aspect of the cook in detail, beginning with the tools and ending with you taking your first bite—a step we refer to as quality control.

As for structure, we could contain some of the preparation steps, such as trimming and seasoning, in separate chapters, but we felt it was easier for the reader to have each meat, be it brisket, ribs, or turkey, be a self-contained unit. This prevents you from flipping around in the book, which not only annoys us as cookbook readers but also could convince you that shortcuts could be taken. This is not our philosophy. If we don't skip any steps, we suggest you don't either.

Here are our ten steps to cooking barbecue in the order that we follow them each week at Goldee's. Each leads to the next, and we recommend following them in order.

Sure, this may sound like strict rules, and perhaps they are. But within this structure there is still space to grow and be creative. Once you have the foundation established, you can build your barbecue meal to suit your personal style.

THE TEN STEPS OF COOKING BARBECUE

STEP 1: TOOLS

For the most part, each cook employs the same tools, which you will learn about in our tool chapter. That said, we do use different knives for trimming, and while you can get away with only having a chef's knife, for instance, if you have a boning knife, we recommend you use it.

STEP 2: MEAT

We'll discuss what to look for when buying the meat for that specific cook. In our meat chapter, we'll go into more detail, but it doesn't hurt to have a short version in front of you as you're looking at the guide for that specific cook.

STEP 3: TRIMMING

Now that you have your tools and your meat, it's time to whip that protein into your ideal shape and get rid of all the extraneous fat and whatnot. We are very specific on these points, and this is not a step that can be shortchanged.

We devote two workdays at the restaurant to trimming our meats, and while you won't be cooking 150 briskets a week, it's sound to set aside the time to get this right. It may be slow in the beginning, but because we want you to do it a certain way each time, the details will be there for you to follow.

STEP 4: SEASONING

Each protein is seasoned in a different way, so we'll be more detailed and tell you whether there's a binder or not, which seasonings and spices we're using, and how we apply them to the meat.

Our application technique, however, does not vary. It doesn't need an entire chapter for an explanation, so here's what we do each time. First, we hold our shaker at eye level with the shaker parallel to the meat. We then rock our wrist back and forth, side to side. This is the position and motion you want to use as you season, as it will help you apply everything more uniformly.

As for the meat, it's easier to season when the long side is facing you. After placing your meat in front of you, position your shaker, and then slowly move down the length of the meat so you can be even in your application.

Once you're done, go back and hit any bald spots, using your hand as a shield so you don't over-apply onto areas that don't need attention. To practice the motion, you can try shaking pepper on a long sheet tray or piece of parchment paper.

For each cook, we'll go into more detail on how many passes to make with each seasoning. One thing that we do at the restaurant is keep each seasoning we use in separate containers, since this is the best way to get a balanced coating of each. Sure, blending them into one bottle appears more efficient, but you will need to keep shaking up the bottle because smaller particles will easily sink to the bottom and the blend won't be balanced.

When we season, our order of application is a binder (if we are using one), black pepper, table salt, then seasoned salt. Pepper *always* goes before the salts because we've found that it doesn't adhere as well if it goes on top of the salt. And then you won't build a beautiful bark, which is the dark crust that forms on the meat as it cooks.

The bark is formed when the smoke combines with the pepper, seasonings, and rendered fat, and it not only provides a crunchy contrast to the meat but is also full of flavor from the smoke and seasonings. It's a crucial component to a cooked brisket, and you want to ensure it stays on the meat.

STEP 5: PLACEMENT ON THE SMOKER

How you place your meat on the smoker is important to the result. Things to consider are how far it needs to be from the fire, which end is facing the fire, and where the doors and walls are. We also talk about what we do to each piece of meat when placing it on the grates. And we give tips on what to do if you're cooking more than one protein, for instance where to place the ribs and brisket if you're doing a cook with both.

STEP 6: FIRE AND SMOKE

We'll cover fire management in greater detail in its namesake chapter, but each cook warrants a slightly different approach. We'll discuss what types of fires we'll be building, and what to do with your damper and door.

STEP 7: TIME AND TEMPERATURE

Each cook has a ballpark time frame and also a recommended set of temperatures that we aim for. That said, there is always leeway, and we don't want you to freak out if your smoker is a few degrees off from the target. This is just a guide, and you will have some wiggle room.

We'll also give you an idea of what to look for along the way. The best pitmaster will use all five senses, not just a thermometer. We want you to be a more confident cook and be able to look at a rack of pork ribs and know that they're ready to pull. We use our thermometers more as probes for doneness rather than looking at the temperatures they announce. Following our descriptions and details will help you do the same.

STEP 8: PULL, WRAP, AND REST

Much like tracking how the meat changes throughout the cook, we can look at the meat, poke it, and have a good idea that it's ready to pull. After you pull the meat, we'll discuss what to do next, such as wrapping it with a sauce, butter, or tallow.

Each meat can rest for different lengths of time, and we'll go into these details. We'll also discuss ways to hold your meats for long periods if that's something you want to do to have a more regular serving schedule. If we recommend a cooler, for instance, we'll cover that in the tools section, so there will be no surprises.

STEP 9: CUT

You're getting closer! Your meat has rested, and it's now ready to be cut and served. We cut each piece differently, so we'll guide you on how best to do it. While you may not be using a tray to display your offerings as we do at the restaurant, we have a sidebar that shows how to arrange a tray in case this is something you wish to do. It's an art that never fails to impress!

STEP 10: QUALITY CONTROL

Before each service, we prepare a full tray of our entire menu and then the team gathers and eats. For the most part, it's a fun step because if you're like us, you love barbecue. Finally savoring the fruits of your labor is a satisfying reward.

That said, we are always challenging ourselves to be better. We analyze all our cooks and gauge what went well and what could be improved. On rare occasions, we even have had to pull an item because it did not meet our standards. But if you've followed all the steps, this will be a joyful moment for you and your guests.

STYLES OF TEXAS BARBECUE

As with all things concerning barbecue, there are multiple theories and opinions about how many styles can be found in Texas. Here is what we consider the four most prominent types of Texas barbecue.

CENTRAL TEXAS: For most, this is the epitome of Texas barbecue. It is rooted in the Central Texas meat market tradition established by Eastern European immigrants to this area of the state in the late 1800s. The meat is seasoned with salt and pepper. It is also sliced versus roughly chopped. This style is cooked indirectly on an offset smoker. Post oak wood is used to fuel the cook. Brisket, pork ribs, and sausage are the three most common meat offerings, along with white bread, pickles, and onions. Sauces and side dishes are now common additions but came about in the later twentieth century as a concession to customers' requests.

EAST TEXAS: Chopped meats are the main event in this region, with an emphasis on pork served with plenty of sauce. Plates and sandwiches are the predominant orders. Offset smokers are still used, but hickory wood, which is sharper, sweeter, and more pungent than post oak, is the wood of choice. East Texas barbecue is rooted in African American Southern barbecue traditions, with its emphasis on chopped meats, pork, and sauce.

SOUTH TEXAS: The southern part of Texas runs along the Texas-Mexican border, and this style of barbecue leans heavily on Texas-Mexican influences such as cooking cuts like cow tongue, beef cheeks, or even an entire cow's head in underground pits. While home cooks may still cook in this fashion, only Vera's Backyard BBQ in Brownsville has been allowed by Texas state regulators to still cook with this ancient method in a commercial setting. Other spots use more traditional smokers instead.

WEST TEXAS: While indirect cooking is prominent throughout the state, the hallmark of the West Texas style is its use of direct heat. The meat is cooked directly over the coals instead of having a heat exchange between a firebox outside the smoker. Mesquite, which grows abundantly throughout this arid part of the state, is the preferred wood. Mesquite's thin logs burn fast and have a potent flavor.

3 PIT ROOM AND

ANTRY

"Are you Goldee?" said a man to a middle-aged woman with white hair pushing a broom across the pit room floor. She laughed, said that she wasn't, and explained that Goldee was a truck, not a person. While the woman was old enough to be the young owners' mother, she was actually an apprentice, learning how to cook barbecue.

When the apprentice had arrived for her first shift at Goldee's early that morning, it was still dark outside and she had envisioned building fires, slicing briskets, and stuffing sausages. There was so much to learn. Lane, the pitmaster on duty, had other ideas.

After offering her some coffee, he handed her a broom and asked her to sweep the pit room. It didn't matter that the apprentice had a long career in food. Everyone is treated the same at Goldee's. If you're there to learn how to make barbecue, then you begin where everyone else has started the journey—with a broom, keeping the pit room clean.

Fortunately there is plenty to do, and the luxury of having a person only on cleaning duty is not a reality. After she finished her job, Lane gave her an apron to wear. He led her back into the kitchen and gave her a tour of all the pantry ingredients and tools. He handed her a pot, gestured toward the spice shelf, and asked her to help make a pot of beans.
As she began learning how the pit room and kitchen operated, she was surprised to see that most of the tools and ingredients on hand were items she had at home. The building blocks for preparing barbecue were familiar and accessible.

When people start getting into cooking barbecue, often they start going on shopping sprees, thinking that the latest gadget or whatnot will help them produce the best smoked meats. Feel free to spend your money as you wish, but here is our essential list of tools.

We use these items every day, and most of them can be found at any decent kitchen shop or restaurant supply. Heck, we've even picked up plenty of these items at the grocery store. Our point is this: You don't need anything fancy or complicated. This basic list will provide you with everything you require.

OUR ESSENTIAL TOOLS

BAKING DISH

A 9-by-13-inch baking dish is required for our bread pudding. You may have one already on hand, but if not, we don't care if you go with a Pyrex one from the grocery store or an old cast-iron one from your grandmother's collection. Whatever works for you is good with us.

BLENDER OR IMMERSION BLENDER

At the restaurant, we use a professional immersion blender that's the size of a small child. It's a good match with our equally tall stock pots. At home, unless you're feeding a crowd, you most likely need a smaller device. An immersion blender is a motor attached to a stick with mixing blades, and we prefer it because you can stick it in the pot and get your puree done without messing with transferring hot liquids to a blender jar. But if you don't have one, a regular stand-up blender will work too. Yes, the fancier the blender, the easier it is to make a puree, but if you're still rocking a harvest gold 1979 Oster and it gets the job done, we approve.

BONING KNIFE

A boning knife, as the name implies, is a thin, sharp blade that is designed for precision work. This is the tool we use when trimming briskets. It's sharp enough to slice off large portions of meat and delicate enough to finesses the right amount of fat off the lean.

BREAD PAN

At the restaurant, we use Ikea bread pans. We were able to buy stacks of them for little money and they've proven to be durable. However, any 9-by-5-inch bread pan will bake our white bread recipe to lofty heights and buttery perfection.

BROOM

Nothing fancy, just something to keep the floor free from soot, ashes, and other stuff.

BUTCHER PAPER

You can buy this by the roll at many Texas grocery stores, such as HEB. You can also find it at restaurant supply stores. These days, we mainly use butcher paper for lining trays and wrapping meats to go, and for signs throughout the restaurant. The latter is especially crucial since it's a challenge writing "Sold Out!" on a piece of foil. It doesn't feel quite the same.

CHEF'S KNIFE

When you see a chef's knife, you think of the platonic ideal of a knife. It's thick and long, and it has a solid handle. It's an all-purpose tool, and if you were to buy only one knife, this would be the one. We use it for cutting up pork butt and brisket trim when making sausage. We also use it when trimming our pork ribs since extra strength is needed to remove the chine bone from the rack.

COOLER, ROTOMOLDED

A rotomolded cooler is a fabrication that is well insulated and strong. If you've ever used a Yeti hard-sided cooler, then you have experience with a rotomolded cooler. Yes, Yetis are expensive. But there are lots of competitors on the market these days, and if you do your research, you may find a bargain. Of course, a cooler is necessary for keeping beverages chilled, but in barbecue we also use it to hold our meats after cooking so they will stay at a consistent temperature. It's not a dedicated warmer, but it does the job.

CUTTING BOARD

We use plastic 18-by-24-inch cutting boards at the restaurant, as they're large enough to accommodate all the large cuts of meat, such as brisket and a long rack of ribs. Of course, they can be used for vegetables and slicing bread too. Most of us prefer the plastic ones since we are cutting raw meat and plastic is easier to sterilize. Jonny, however, prefers to cut on wood.

DISH TOWELS

You can never have too many dish towels. However, for our purposes, you don't want to get anything too fancy since it's going to be used to mop up blood and wipe down soot and ash.

DUTCH OVEN/STOCKPOT

For our recipes, a 2-gallon Dutch oven or stockpot is the perfect size for making beans, grits, and stock.

HEAT-SAFE GLOVES

At the restaurant, we keep on hand heat-resistant gloves that fit perfectly under the disposable latex gloves we use when cooking. Even if you're not using latex gloves at home, heat-resistant gloves will be a good friend when pulling hot meats off the smoker.

HEAVY-DUTY FOIL

We go through tons of foil and have learned that not all foil is created equal. We recommend you look for foil that says "heavy duty" on the box because the last thing you want to happen when you're wrapping meats is to have that foil pouch burst and all your juices escape.

KNIFE SHARPENER

If you have a fancy knife collection, then you probably have a honing steel. This gets the knife particles all in a row, but if you want to sharpen the blade, you'll need more than that. While there are complicated methods such as using a sharpening stone, at the restaurant we place on the trimming table a few handheld knife sharpeners, which get the job done in a few swipes with no worries about cutting your fingers.

LADLE, 1-CUP

If you get serious about wrapping briskets with an exact amount of tallow, a 1-cup ladle will come in handy. As a bonus, you also can use it to scoop out beans and do other assorted ladling tasks you might have.

LIGHTER

You'll want a long fireplace lighter, the kind that is kid-proof with both a trigger and a switch that you have to operate at the same time. If you've never used one of these lighters, to use it is a bit like rubbing your belly while tapping your head. But once you get coordinated, having its extra reach will come in handy as you start your fires in the firebox.

MEAT GRINDER, ELECTRIC

If you're making sausage, an electric meat grinder is a vital piece of equipment. While you could get the stand-mixer attachment, if you have any desire to make more than one or two batches of sausage, we say go for the upgrade. There are manual grinders, too, but we just don't have time for that. At the restaurant, we use a Cabela grinder. LEM, Weston, and Hobart are other solid brands. When shopping, look for stainless steel construction, the ability to take it apart to clean it, and at least a three-year warranty. It will probably come with a sausage-stuffing attachment, which you can also use, but don't make that your deciding factor.

MEAT THERMOMETER, INSTANT-READ

These days, we're more likely to probe our meats with a thermometer to check for tenderness rather than temperature, but we keep plenty of these around in the pit room and kitchen. A waterproof instant-read thermometer with a backlight is great for our dark and smoky needs. We've used everything from Thermapen to ThermoPro, and they all get the job done. Inevitably, we'll drop it and it will break, so we don't grow too attached.

MESH STRAINER

This is a must if you're rendering tallow so you can separate the liquid gold from the used-up meaty pieces.

RACK

When you buy sheet pans (see below), often you'll have an option to get an inserting rack. If you're making sausage, you'll want this rack. It's good for cooling baked goods too.

SAUSAGE STUFFER

Yes, your stand mixer and meat grinder may have this attachment, but there's a time in every sausage maker's life when they decide to take the leap and go dedicated. You don't have to begin with a 20-pound electronic device, though if you want to spend the money, go for it. Even getting a little 5-pound stand-up stuffer, such as the ones made by LEM, will improve your sausage-making game way beyond using the grinder.

SCALE

This is another must for us. While we still measure in volume for some things, such as our sides, when it comes to baking our bread and making sausages, a scale is necessary. You also can use it to portion out your cooked meats if you like.

SERRATED KNIFE

When we're on the chopping block during service, we're wielding a jagged-edge cutting knife. It's long, it's sharp, and its pointed teeth go through all the meats easily and cleanly. No shreds on our cutting board—with our serrated knife we can slice that barky brisket as easily as cake. A serrated knife may be used to slice up bread too.

SHEET PANS

We love sheet pans. They hold our meats both before they're cooked and after, they're the perfect surface for baking our banana pudding crumble, and they hold our bread pans while the loaves cool.

SHOVEL

You don't need anything fancy. An iron shovel head on a wooden stick will do just fine. We use this to manage the firebox since the iron head can take the heat and the long stick keeps our more delicate hands and arms farther away.

SPRAY BOTTLE

We fill these up with warm water to spritz our meats before seasoning if we're not using a binder.

SQUEEZE BOTTLE

If you're making ribs, this is what you'll use to apply the glaze. Of course, you could use a spoon or a ladle, but holding a squeeze bottle in your hands, especially if you get the souped-up triple-trip version like we have, will make you feel like an artist as you paint your glaze onto the foil.

STAND MIXER

This will make much easier work of making bread and sausage.

WIDE METAL MIXING BOWLS

You can never have too many metal mixing bowls. So why not get a few more?

WHAT'S IN OUR PANTRY

As with our kitchen tools, our pantry ingredients are pretty straightforward. Most of these can be found at any grocery store, and a quick trip online will fill in any gaps.

CHEDDAR CHEESE

At Goldee's, we use sharp yellow cheddar produced by Tillamook. We like its creamy texture and tangy flavor. If you can find this brand, we highly recommend it! Any yellow cheddar cheese will work for our cheese grits recipe.

CHILI POWDER

Texans like to argue about whether the original commercial chili powder was sold by Fort Worth's Pendery's Spices or Gebhardt's, which was started in New Braunfels by a German man. But we give Gebhardt's the edge, with its balance of ancho chili, garlic, and oregano. We're not into keeping secrets, but Lane swears it's why our pinto beans hit so hard.

FLOUR, BREAD

For our loaves of bread, we prefer bread flour. You can use all-purpose flour, too, but bread flour makes for a soft and solid loaf with its additional protein count.

GARLIC, FRESH

We use this sharp aromatic in our sausages and slaw. We go with it instead of garlic powder when we're looking for maximum garlic punch.

GARLIC POWDER

While fresh garlic provides a pop, garlic powder is a more mellow layer of flavor. We spoon it into a wide variety of dishes, such as our seasoned salt, our beans, and our rib glaze.

GRITS

At the restaurant, we love Bob's Red Mill yellow grits, which are often sold under the name polenta at grocery stores. Don't worry, it's the same stone-ground yellow cornmeal. There are three styles of grits—instant, quick, and stone-ground. These are all made from stone-ground corn. There are also hominy grits, which are ground from corn but the corn has been nixtamalized, a process in which the corn is treated with calcium lime, which causes the corn to puff and bloom. This puffed corn is known as hominy, and it has a nuttier flavor than regular corn. (Nixtamalized corn is also the grain used to make corn masa for

tortillas.) Bob's Red Mill straddles that middle ground of being stone-ground medium, which means that the grits have an interesting texture but they don't take a year to cook.

GUAJILLO CHILIES

This fruity, red dried chili is what Lane likes to use in his bowl of Texas red chili. When asked why he chose it over the more prominent ancho chili typically found in commercial chili powder, such as Gebhardt's, and other heritage Texas chili recipes, he said it tasted like home.

JALAPEÑOS

Texas has a state chili pepper, and it's the plump, green, dagger-shaped jalapeño. It's got just enough heat to keep things interesting and has enough flavor to balance out discomfort. It plays a starring role in our jalapeño cheese sausage.

LEMONGRASS, GROUND

Lemongrass is a tall grass that has a zesty flavor like its namesake fruit. For accuracy in our sausage, we started using a ground version, which has a similar essence.

LIME LEAF

Lime leaf, also known as Makrut lime leaf, is a bright and lively Asian herb. It also adds a spark of acidity to our Lao Texas sausage.

MEAT

When choosing our meats, we go with creatures that have been treated humanely and fed healthy diets free of antibiotics. When you use quality meat, the cook will always taste better. For each particular cook, we'll go into what to look for, but we try to get the best that we can afford, which is better for the environment and for our bellies.

MILK POWDER, LOW-FAT

Milk powder is shelf-stable milk solids that have had the liquid removed. In making sausage, we use it as a binder. We recommend low-fat powder because we don't want to add any extra fat to our recipe. Fortunately, most milk powders sold at the grocery store are low fat, though if you have trouble sourcing it you can get it online.

ONION POWDER

This white ground aromatic is a secret weapon. It's loaded with the savory flavor known as umami and brings an addictive layer of flavor wherever it's added. Keep it away from moisture, though, as it tends to clump easily.

ONIONS, YELLOW AND RED

We use fresh onions in our side dishes, both yellow and red varieties.

COARSE BLACK PEPPER

Our black pepper is coarsely ground to a size known as 16-mesh. This means that the pepper grains are coarse enough to go through a mesh screen with sixteen openings per inch. It's not the coarsest grind, but it's also not too fine. It's the perfect size for seasoning our meats with the control we seek, and its coarse grounds also add a hit of heat to our sides.

PINK CURING SALT

There are two kinds of pink curing salts, which are also called Prague powder, and they are known as number one and number two. We use number one exclusively in our sausages, so that's the one you want. We'll go into more detail in our sausage chapter, but number one is a blend of table salt and nitrites; number two also has nitrates. Nitrates are designed to keep uncooked cured meats from spoiling, and we're cooking our meats, so we only need the nitrites to keep the meat safe as we cold smoke it for several hours.

PINTO BEANS

When Texans cook beans, most likely they're cooking a pot of pintos. It's a meaty legume that holds its own against bold flavors such as chopped beef and chili powder. And its oval shape is what we strive to achieve when we trim our briskets. You will find these everywhere, and we don't recommend any particular brand, though you want dried pinto beans. It's best to purchase from a store that sells a lot so their inventory will be fresh.

RED CHILI FLAKES, KOREAN

We love the sharp, sweet, mild heat these bring to our side dishes. They also add a pop of color to our yellow cheese grits. If you can't find these, pizza-style dried red chilies or ground chiles de árbol can work too.

SALT

In the beginning, we were firmly on team kosher salt when it came to seasoning our meats. However, over time, we began to appreciate how the finer grains of table salt are more adhesive to the meat, and we now use it exclusively for our barbecue. For our side dishes, we go back and forth.

For you as a cook, always use table salt when seasoning the meats since it will give you better coverage; coarse-ground salts such as kosher may not adhere as well. For cooking, our recipes call for kosher salt, which will create a less salty taste because it's lighter than table salt. If you want to substitute table salt in our recipes, cut the amount of kosher salt called for in half, then taste and make adjustments. We use Morton salts at the restaurant.

SAUSAGE CASING

For our sausages, because we're only making one style, we use exclusively 32-to-38-millimeter pork casing. You can find these at a butcher and easily order them online.

SHALLOTS

This member of the onion family produces a sweet and savory flavor that is more gentle than that of white onions. We use it in our Lao Texas sausage.

THAI CHILIES, FRESH

These tiny daggers produce a ton of heat. Most often these will still be green, but sometimes you find some fresh red ones, and if you do, know that they may pack more heat. If you can't find fresh Thai chilies, you can use a serrano chili instead.

PITMASTER PROFILE

LANE MILNE

Lane was stressed. No, scratch that—Lane *is* stressed. Every single day, Lane worries over how to make Goldee's a better experience for all. But that's okay; he seems to like it. He keeps the rambling train running, and no matter how close to the edge a situation may travel, Lane will easily pull it back into a more safe and chill zone. He's incredible in a crisis.

Lane was once crowned the sausage king of Austin, and he also has the nickname "the Flavor Scientist." Both of these point to Lane's genius approach to food. He can taste a bit of anything and know what the ingredients are and how it was prepared, and if it's an homage, he'll share its lineage with you too.

For instance, one time we were eating sausages at a local barbecue spot. There was one with peppers and cheese, but the cheese was French, not the usual American or English. Lane identified everything and then began to discuss the evolution of cheese in sausages across Texas. Even if he hadn't eaten one yet, he would have been well versed in its details. So much so that he had already tasted it in his mind. It was fully formed in his imagination.

Lane is our master teacher. If you have the opportunity to work with him one-on-one, know that you're working with the best. He's patient and kind, and while he can be exacting, he softens everything he says with his inquisitive and hilarious banter. Hanging out with Lane in the kitchen and pit room is always a blast.

If you're patient, you will learn more than you ever thought possible about how ingredients play well together, how to read a fire, and how to maximize the flavor from the fewest ingredients. Lane can do anything, and he's happy to share all of his knowledge with you.

Once you pass these early tests, Lane begins to relax. You'll even get to see Lane smile. And a smile from Lane is the best reward since it's filled with such light and joy. People have even asked if he's the reason why the restaurant is called Goldee's, since happy Lane has such a golden glow.

MEAT GRADES

When it comes to beef, there are three main grades you will be faced with when you are making your purchase at a grocery or big-box store. These grades are determined by the United States Department of Agriculture (USDA), and they are based on the projected tenderness and juiciness of the cut, along with how much usable meat will be available after cooking. These grades are a standardized way for the customer to make an informed choice as they prepare to cook.

PRIME: Prime is the highest grade of beef. With prime cuts, expect plenty of fat woven into the lean. Fat is the carrier for both juice and flavor in a cut of beef, so the expectation is that a prime cut will have more of both. This distribution of fat to meat is known as marbling, which is because a well-marbled piece of meat looks like the stone from which it gets its name. This beef comes from younger, well-fed cows. Likewise, more fat means that the muscles were less worked, which also improves the cooked quality of the meat.

CHOICE: While still a high-quality grade, there is less fat distribution here, therefore its grade is lower since the expectation is that the meat could be less juicy than the prime. These cuts typically come from the loin and the ribs. Choice, however, despite not being the highest grade, still yields juicy, tender cooked beef. Indeed, we use choice-grade briskets at the restaurant, which we will go into more in the brisket chapter.

SELECT: The lack of heavy marbling in this grade means that the meat-to-fat ratio is higher. Because there's more tough meat and less tender fat, the meat is predicted to be less juicy and flavorful. However, one can still coax plenty of flavor and tenderness from this cut.

4 SMOKERS

Even though it was April, Jonny was like a kid at Christmas with his latest acquisition—a backyard smoker that he had designed. For the past few years, after cooking on a variety of offset pits—from rusting backyard rigs to tightly welded 1,000-gallon bullets—he had pondered how to improve the classic offset pit.

When he came up with a blueprint for how to mitigate the chance of fire entering the small cooking chamber, Jonny bought welding equipment, found a 250-gallon propane tank, and began working on his dream. This was in the easygoing summer of 2021, but soon, he would be too busy to continue. The unfinished pit began to gather cobwebs in Jonny's backyard.

Anyone who talked to him, though, would get to hear his big idea. He'd pull out a marker, grab a sheet of butcher paper, and draw his design. Its curves looked more like surrealist architecture than Central Texas barbecue, but he finally found a fabricator to build his vision, and everyone was excited to see this new pit come to life.

Around Easter, the new pit arrived. That week, one apprentice cooked the juiciest brisket of her life and then Jalen made juicy, succulent ribs on the new Goldee's pit. It was a joy to cook on such a thoughtful design.

While you don't have to start out with our smoker, before you can cook proper Texas barbecue, you will need a way to cook with smoke. There are a variety of live-fire cooking devices available, but we use offset smokers at Goldee's. This is the standard cooker found in Central Texas barbecue, and it's what we've been cooking with since we started. We understand its quirks and charms, and we love the flavor and tenderness it can produce.

But if you don't know anything about smokers, then the term *offset* may mean nothing. Let us explain. An offset smoker means that the fire is separate from the cooking chamber. The heat it produces is indirect. Unlike a grill, for instance, where you place the meat on a rack directly over the fire, which would make that direct heat, an offset smoker has a cooking chamber filled with only grates; the fire is not in the cooking chamber. It's offset, or offsite.

We're not scientists, so we're not going to go into too much detail about how the smoke moves from the firebox to the chamber and beyond. We do know, however, that heat rises, so naturally the smoke will lift out of the firebox. We also know that the smokestack and damper, which make up that tall pole on the other end of the cooking chamber, pulls the smoke, heat, and air through the chamber.

If you've ever smoked a pipe, for instance, its airflow is quite similar to that of an offset smoker. First, you have your combustible material at one end. Then, there's a hollow tube that is connected to that chamber. Finally, your mouth is the damper, and as you inhale, the lit tobacco gathers more heat and smoke and your lungs pull that smoke into your mouth.

Now, we're not suggesting that you go out and start smoking. However, we've noticed that the concept of cooking on an offset smoker can be quite foreign to those who've only cooked either in a kitchen oven or even on a grill. While it can get a bit complicated, there's no reason to overthink using a smoker. You'll soon learn it's no more challenging than a large oven.

On most offset smokers, you have a firebox, which is where you place your logs. There's a door on the firebox, which is one means of controlling the airflow of a smoker. In between the firebox and the cooking chamber is what some refer to as the exchange. This is the opening that allows the heat and smoke to travel up from the firebox into the chamber. And notice we said to travel *up*. This is because the firebox is positioned lower than the chamber since the natural flow of heat and smoke is upward.

While having to bend to insert those logs may be a bit harder on your back, it wouldn't be very efficient to have the firebox at the same level as the cooking chamber. First, as we said, the goal is to cook indirectly.

Lane has a trick where he'll open the cooking chamber doors and place his head at meat level. If he can't see the flames in the firebox, then the meat can't either. This is a good thing since it means the only things hitting the meat are smoke and heat. Flames cause the meat to singe and burn.

Then there's the nature of physics. As we said, we don't know the formulas behind why these things are the way they are, but if the firebox were above the cooking chamber, for instance, the smoke and heat would be bouncing around and inefficiently moving from the box into the chamber. It wouldn't work.

Fireboxes can come in a few shapes, such as square or round. Everyone has a preference, but you ultimately want the shape that works for you. For instance, some feel it's easier to build a lower fire in a square firebox, while others feel that the curved walls of a round firebox promote better airflow.

Then there are insulated versus non-insulated fireboxes. The advantage of the insulated firebox is that it retains heat and your logs will last much longer. To us, however, this is also the disadvantage of the insulated firebox, since slower-burning logs means a lot less smoke and flavor. We'd rather feed the firebox and have our meats taste and look as we want them to than the alternative.

After your firebox, you have the cooking chamber. Today, this is usually a cylindrical shape. The reason for this is that many offset smokers were fashioned out of old propane tanks, though when you visit some older restaurants, you'll see square pits built out of bricks, which is how they were originally done. Smitty's in Lockhart, which was built in 1924, has its fire not even contained in a box but simply on the ground close to the pit. That's truly offset!

The size of the cooking chamber will determine how much you're able to cook. At the restaurant, we use two 1,000-gallon offset smokers for our briskets. We also use our backyard 94-gallon offset for our turkeys, and then we have a 2,000-gallon offset rotisserie. Most modern BBQ restaurants using offset smokers are working with the cylindrical 1,000-gallon, like what we have for our briskets. It's what we trained on when we were working at restaurants in Austin, and you see them everywhere.

We've produced plenty of excellent cooks on these workhorses, though there are limitations. For instance, because of the way the heat enters the cooking chamber from the firebox, the first few feet of the smoker can't be used for true offset smoking—it's too hot and the flames can sometimes find their way into the chamber.

If you're looking at a 1,000-gallon smoker, for instance, you'll notice that it usually has four doors. At Goldee's, we don't even bother with the first door since we know that we're not going to be using that space to cook (though you can use the front grate in the smoker for hotter cooks, such as chicken). Some smoker manufacturers don't even bother putting a cooking grate behind that first door without charging extra for it since no pitmaster in their right mind would use it.

As you can see, this is a limitation of the offset smoker. To say it could contain 1,000 gallons is not true because you're eliminating one-quarter of your cooking space. We'll get back to that in a minute, but it's something to keep in mind.

If you're using an offset smoker in your backyard, for instance, it's usually a size of 90 to 95 gallons. If it's a traditionally designed one, then that doesn't leave you much true offset cooking space, since you need to position your meats as far from the exchange/firebox as possible.

One solution to maximize cooking space is inserting a double rack, though we're not fans of this. When you have one rack above another, the meats cooking on the upper rack will drip onto the meats below. This will affect bark formation and the evenness of your cook. It's not worth it to us.

Another solution is a mechanism called reverse flow. Now, we've never cooked on one of these, but from what we understand, there's a plate under the grates that creates a separate chamber underneath the chamber where you place the meats. The damper, which controls the flow of air, is not opposite the firebox but instead above it.

In a reverse flow, the heat enters this subchamber, travels underneath, and then exits at the opposite end. While this does keep the flames from entering the cooking chamber, we hear that it can become incredibly hot underneath the meats, so it's not a perfect solution.

Since we've already started talking about smokestacks and dampers, we'll now go into more detail about these components. The smokestack in a traditional offset smoker is opposite the firebox at the other end of the cooking chamber. It's where the smoke and heat exit the smoker. The damper, which is a moveable flat disk on top of the smokestack, is the means for you to control the pull of the flow, which is determined by the width of the smokestack opening.

What does this mean? Well, if the damper is all the way open, and the smokestack exit is wide, then the pull will be greater. The heat and smoke will enter the chamber but because the pull of the smokestack is so strong, the heat and smoke will zoom right through the chamber. It won't linger. The advantage of this is that your fires will burn strong. The disadvantage is that you'll go through more logs, the meat won't taste as smoky, and the cook will take much longer.

If you adjust the damper, however, you can slow down the flow and let the heat and smoke hang out in the cooking chamber for a bit. Not only does this create a better bark but the meat will taste like it's been cooked with smoke. It will also allow the meat to cook at a faster rate since the heat is more concentrated.

At Goldee's, we prefer to keep the damper halfway open. This is for efficiency because having this one variable stay constant allows us to control our cooks better. That said, we advise you to start your cook with the damper fully open, which helps your initial fires in a clean, cold firebox to burn faster and build your coal bed.

After your first one or two fires, you should have a decent bed of coals to set your new logs on. These coals will help the fresh logs catch and you won't need the smokestack's assistance. At this point, we then close the damper halfway, which traps just enough heat and smoke in the cooking chamber to cook in a timely manner and build a beautiful bark.

Let's go back to the cooking chamber. On the walls with the doors, there will probably be at least one temperature gauge. This tells you what the temperature is at that position of the chamber, and if it's in the center of the chamber, you have a good average temperature.

Know that the heat of the chamber is not equal in all places. For instance, it's warmer closer to the firebox and closer to the smokestack. It's also warmer by the walls and doors versus in the center of the racks. This is because the heat gets trapped in all these locations.

When we're placing briskets on our offsets, for instance, we place the larger ones back by the smokestack and along the walls. The smaller ones, which will take less time to cook, go in the center. Now, on a backyard smoker, since you won't be cooking twenty-four briskets, this won't be a typical problem for you to solve. But the heat accumulation pattern is the same, so you'll want to position your meats accordingly if you are cooking more than one item. (When you get into the cooking portion of the book, each of our smoked meat recipes will give more detail about where we recommend placing the meat.)

One way of getting to know your smoker is by doing what is known as the biscuit test. This is where you position raw biscuits in your smoker, you fire it up, and then after an hour or so you can look at the now-cooked biscuits and tell where your hot spots are by their color. If the biscuits are burnt in one spot, then you know you have a hot spot. If your biscuits are just right, then that's a safe place to put your meat.

Before you use your smoker, you'll want to season it. It's like a cast-iron skillet. By coating it all over, inside and out, with spray cooking oil and then running a fire, the metal will cure and get a patina. This helps prevent rust since there's a lot of liquid in the smoke. It will also make it easier to clean.

Cleaning day at Goldee's is a necessary part of the job. We deep clean our smokers once a month. After cleaning them, they look brand new. It's a long day, and the work is dirty and messy, but you must do it. If you don't clean your smoker, the gunk will build up inside and mess with the airflow. This will affect the evenness of your cooks, so it's necessary. But it's not fun.

To clean our smokers, we first remove all the grates. They're heavy and that's hard work. Then we get in each smoker with a power washer and keep spraying until everything is broken down and washed out. We do the same for the grates. There's no technique really: It's just spray and clean. If you do it often enough, the buildup won't be too bad, but you must do it.

We don't reseason the smokers after washing them since there's enough of an oil patina on the inside and the grates already. Our first cook will add plenty of oil too. If you're using a new smoker, though, and it doesn't already have that oil-coated surface, you may want to spray it with cooking spray before cooking again.

Your smoker will most likely have a drain hole for all the fats, and as this fills up, you'll need to dump out this fat. This gets rid of a lot of the excess, but it doesn't remove everything. You'll still need to deep clean the chamber too.

Okay, so we've talked about the standard offset smoker design, which works. But after years of cooking, we had some ideas about how to improve things. The most important issue we found was the firebox exchange.

As we said, in the traditional design you lose so much cooking real estate because the fire is still too close to the chamber. It's not truly offset until you're a distance away from the firebox. We wondered if this could be solved in some way.

Jonny came up with a design and spoke to a physics professor. His idea was to have a 90-degree tube between the firebox and the chamber so that the heat and smoke would travel through this before reaching the chamber. The idea was that this journey through the tube would keep the flames, which cause direct heat, in the firebox and not the chamber. In turn, you would have more cooking real estate in the chamber.

After he drew up his plans, he shared them with Mike Miller Jr., the owner of the smoker fabricator M&M BBQ Company in Tool, Texas, and it was built. On our smoker, we also raised the height of the smokestack so that there would be sufficient draw of the heat. It may look unusual, but we were thrilled to learn that it works very well.

When we did our biscuit test (see sidebar), we noticed that in the smoker the only hot spots were at the point where the tube entered the chamber. So it's not perfect, but instead of losing almost a third of our cooking space, we now lose only a small square portion.

There is also a hot spot close to the smokestack, but again, it's minor and not any more significant than a traditional offset. What does this mean? Well, in a traditional backyard smoker, you probably wouldn't be able to cook more than three briskets, for instance. In ours, you can easily cook six. So right there, we're doubling our cooking capacity in the same amount of space!

Jonny also had M&M etch lines on the damper for the different positions, such as one-fourth open, one-half open, and three-fourths open. This way we know exactly where to move it depending on what we're trying to achieve. It helps us be more accurate in dialing in our cooks. It's a huge advantage because we've been known to climb up on the roof with a ruler to determine exactly where to position our dampers, but with these engraved lines, we only have to line it up—no ruler or climbing is necessary!

We now use our backyard smoker at the restaurant to cook our boneless turkey breasts. We use it only for turkeys because our other smokers are filled with briskets and ribs. This allows us to cook our turkeys the way we want instead of having to cook them according to the brisket or rib specs. But we've used it to cook briskets for service too! Not to toot our own horn, but it's the best damn backyard smoker we've ever used, and it has everything we need to cook a Texas number-one brisket, rack of ribs, turkey, or whatever we choose.

At the restaurant, we also have a rotisserie. It's not gas-assisted, but it does have electronic dampers to control the temperature. The firebox sits low, and much like our backyard offset, there's a tube pulling the heat and smoke into the chamber, and the flames stay in the box. We love it because the heat is super even in there. The rotation of the racks also

Placing meats on our rotisserie smoker.

helps with this evenness of the cook. Currently, there's not much of a market for backyard rotisseries, but they do solve many of the issues that pitmasters face with an offset.

Before we had the rotisserie, we were smoking around the clock. Now we can get some sleep because instead of needing to come in at midnight after we've pulled the briskets to load the smokers with ribs, we can come in at 4:00 a.m. The hours are still long, but psychologically, we feel as if it's made our lives much easier.

Of course, some say that because rotisserie smokers are electronic, it's not a purist approach to barbecue. We understand that, but if you're cooking in a restaurant and need to produce meat in a high volume, as we do, it's a good solution.

And since there's no gas assist with ours, which is made by M&M, who also produces our custom offset, the heat is still coming only from wood. We still cook only the briskets on the offsets, though, and do only ribs and pork bellies on the rotisserie.

One more thing we'd like to mention. Jonny once built an offset smoker out of cinder blocks (see sidebar). Sure, it's not fancy, but it gets the job done! If you're itching to cook barbecue but on a budget, it's not a bad place to start!

COOKING WITHOUT AN OFFSET SMOKER

We are offset smoker guys, and that's all we've cooked with for as long as we've been in barbecue. Our instructions are specific to this style of smoker, yet we are aware that not everyone has access to one of these in their backyard.

During the course of writing this book, we had recipe testers who used pellet grills and kettle grills to smoke our recipes. They reported great success applying our methods to their specific cooker.

That said, we are not well versed in this type of live-fire cooking, so we're not informed enough to give you instructions tailored to other types of cookers. We're sorry, but we have never cooked any other way!

However, if you want to improve your home-kitchen meat skills, know that all of our smoker recipes can also be cooked in a home oven. Sure, you won't get a smoky flavor, but your meats will be tender and juicy with a savory, crisp bark.

CINDER BLOCK OFFSET SMOKER

When we returned to North Texas to open Goldee's, we all lived at Nupohn's house in the nearby town of Irving. It had been his parents' house, and when they moved they let the guys live there rent free. In the backyard were stacks of cinder blocks to build a whole hog smoker. After we were done with that, Jonny had the idea to reposition them into an offset smoker.

He went out and moved the blocks around until it worked and he was happy with the design. What's cool about it is that it doesn't cost a lot and the materials are available all over the world. His goal was to bring barbecue to everyone and show them how they could have a good offset smoker. And it works really well too!

If you're in a money crunch (or time crunch, considering some of the better backyard smoker welders can take over a year to deliver), this is a good way to get started and begin practicing. It's super cool, super efficient, and super easy to make!

45 cinder blocks
25 bricks
4 (48-inch) flat metal bars
2 (24 x 24-inch) metal grates
1 (48 x 48-inch) piece of wood
1 (36 x 36-inch) piece of metal (bent in half)
A smoker thermometer, such as one made by Tel-Tru
A drill

Clear off a 6-foot patch of cement or grass.

Start the first layer by laying down three cinder blocks, with the two end block holes facing up and the block in the middle with the holes facing out. The middle one will be part of the firebox.

To complete the first layer, place five blocks down, with the holes up, on both sides of the first row. Complete the rectangle by laying down three more blocks, all with the holes up.

Repeat for the second layer, except place all the blocks with the holes up.

Now, to build the firebox, go inside the rectangle. One block's width away from the firebox side, place one block standing vertically, with the holes pointing toward the middle.

Place another block beside it, but position it horizontally, like the block walls are placed, with the holes facing up.

Place the final block on the other side of the middle block, again standing vertically, with the holes facing the middle. These three blocks should now form a U shape.

Now, to complete the firebox inside the rectangle, take another block and place it horizontally on top of the center block, with the holes facing out, like the first-row block on the outside was placed.

Take the bricks and arrange them the best you can between the interior firebox and the adjacent wall, where the firebox block is placed. Now your firebox is complete!

Take the four metal bars and lay them flat, equidistant across the top of the remaining interior on the other side of the firebox. Place the grates on top of the metal bars.

Now, take eight cinder blocks, place two down on the firebox end, holes facing up, and then place the remaining three on each side, again with the holes facing up.

On the open side, you're going to build the smokestack. Over the center cinder block, place three bricks horizontally, with the holes facing up.

Pushed up against the sides of the three-brick stack, place a cinder block horizontally, holes up, on each side of the brick tower, with no gaps. There will be a little outside gap on each side of the cinder blocks, but that's okay.

Now, in the center, on top of the brick stack, lay down a vertical stack of three cinder blocks, all on top of each other, with the holes facing up. This stack of bricks and cinder blocks is your smokestack.

You now have a firebox, a cooking chamber, and a smokestack.

On the board, drill a hole in the center and screw in the thermometer.

Lay the board with the thermometer over the cooking chamber.

Now, take the metal folded in half and lay it over the firebox.

To manage the fire, lift the metal firebox cover. You'll be building fires from above instead of using a shovel to feed the firebox horizontally, as you'd normally do in a welded offset.

Other than that, it's the same technique! And that's it! Now you can lay down your logs, load your meat on the rack, and use the smoker like you'd use any other offset smoker!

THE BISCUIT TEST

When pitmasters buy a new smoker, they use a method known as the biscuit test to see where the hot spots are in the cooking chamber. While we're not sure of the exact origin of this genius idea, people started discussing it online in smoked meat forums around 2007.

To do the biscuit test is simple. You take raw biscuit dough, form it into biscuits, place them on your smoker, then fire it up and see how they cook. Burnt biscuits will let you know that you have a hot spot. Biscuits that are golden and attractive will show a safe cooking zone.

Most people use canned biscuits for the biscuit test. They are quick to use: You just pop open a can or two, and you're ready to cook. If you're feeling more ambitious, though, we've also provided you with a biscuit recipe (see page 222) that uses tallow. It's a fine, flaky biscuit, and if you like the flavor of a smoky biscuit, they'll work just fine.

Here's what you need to do on a backyard smoker. If you're working with a larger chamber, just use more biscuits!

16 raw biscuits, already cut
A smoker
Enough logs to run a 275°F fire

Place the biscuits in your smoker. We recommend doing four rows with four biscuits each, but you can arrange them however you like. Just make sure you have a good distribution from end to end so you can gauge your hot spots accurately.

Fire up your smoker and run it at about 275°F. Run your fire for about an hour, checking on the biscuits after half an hour to see how they're doing.

After the biscuits are done, examine them to find which ones are burnt and which ones are golden. Throw out the burnt ones. You might want to throw out the golden ones, too, though some folks enjoy the smoky taste.

5 WOOD AND FIRE

If you walk into the pit room while we're cooking, you will inevitably see at least one of the team tending the fire. Everyone at Goldee's has been taught to grade logs, read flames, manage temperatures, and control the flow of smoke. There are no secrets in fire management, and you just need to start building fires to understand them.

Some have more experience than others. One chilly afternoon, one apprentice was trying to get a fire ignited in one of the backyard smokers, but it kept coughing smoke back out the wrong end. Nupohn walked by and pointed to her damper, which was halfway closed. "Open your damper all the way," he said. "The extra pull from the smokestack will be enough to ignite the wood." She opened the damper all the way, and he was correct. Her fire sparked.

That same day, young pit hand Joseph was tending to the 500-gallon smoker, and he had arranged his logs at an interesting angle. It wasn't the standard formation, but his flames were low and it seemed to get the job done.

At the other end of the pit room, cooks Kim and Cecilia each had control of one of the 1,000-gallon pits. Like the Greek goddess Hestia, who manages the hearth on Mount Olympus, the two were each sitting by their respective fireboxes, keeping an eye on the flames.

Kim was decked in standard cook attire—camouflage pants, a barbecue T-shirt, and comfortable shoes. Cecilia, however, followed her own sartorial path, which included a long, flowing skirt topped with a Goldee's shirt trimmed *Flashdance* style. Each fire, like the person tending it, was unique, which shows there's not one way to present or behave as a pitmaster. Just come as you are.

Low and slow is our approach to fire management in an offset smoker. Because we're cooking with indirect heat, we want our fires to reflect this. Some may think that the phrase refers to the temperature and time of the cook, but for us, low and slow refers to how our fires behave in the firebox.

For instance, an inefficient or fast fire is one where the flames are tall and moving around wildly. They might even reach through the exchange and throw sparks into the cooking chamber. For our style of cooking, this doesn't work because it cooks everything too quickly and will burn the meat.

If you have an efficient fire, you're in control. The flames are low and are contained in the firebox. They're giving off heat but not ripping into the cooking chamber. And their slow and contained combustion means that your meat will cook more evenly. This is our goal.

There's a lot to understand about building a fire, so we're going to walk you through everything we know: the wood we use, its characteristics, styles of fires, and how to control your fire. Fire management can be intimidating, but once you start building fires, it becomes a lot easier to understand. Hopefully, our guidance will help!

TYPES OF WOOD AND THEIR CHARACTERISTICS

Let's start with wood. At Goldee's we use post oak. This is the classic choice of Central Texas–style barbecue because post oak trees are abundant in the central part of the state. It's a thick, barky wood, and its density works for our long cooks. We also enjoy the flavor of post oak, which is subtle and mild.

Hickory, another thick wood used in other barbecue regions, also burns slowly, but its flavor is too sharp and sweet. We're not fans. Post oak, however, has a mild flavor that doesn't overpower the meat.

Some people are fans of the tangy, sweet flavors from mesquite and fruit woods, but they're just too thin to be used in abundance. You'd need to pair them with thicker logs; otherwise you'd be building twice as many fires. Mesquite's flavor can also turn acrid if used for too long, so even though it grows all over South Texas, it doesn't work for us and our style of barbecue.

If you want to use mesquite or fruit wood for a layer of flavor, we recommend using it only for the first few hours. That's when the meats are raw, and it's at that point in the cook that it's taking on a lot of that smoked flavor. For those first few hours, if you use a different type of wood, you will be able to taste it. You can then finish the rest of the cook with a wood that burns longer and holds its temperature.

GREEN VERSUS DRY LOGS

Another key factor to consider with your wood is whether it's green or dry. *Green* doesn't necessarily refer to its color; instead, it is wood that has a higher water content. It's usually more freshly cut, and because it has more moisture, it's going to be slow to catch fire and will also give off way more smoke.

Dry logs, as the name implies, are dry or without much internal moisture. They either have been sitting in the sun for longer or have been put into an oven called a kiln to speed up the drying process. Kiln-dried wood is especially efficient and catches fire in no time. Though it's easier to burn fires with it, you will end up using more because it has so little moisture.

When assessing your wood pile, your greener logs will be heavier. They may even still feel damp to the touch. Your drier logs will be lighter and will feel papery to the touch. If you've paid for kiln-dried logs, then you'll know that they're very dry. If you want to get scientific, there are devices to test the water density of a log, but we don't mess with those. We just go by how they feel in our hands and their weight.

If your log pile is exposed to wet weather, you can light a fire in your smoker and then place the wet logs on the grates. We've had to do this after winter storms when the entire pile was buried in snow. You can leave them on to evaporate the excess moisture.

Don't get us wrong, though: Green logs do have their place! Because they give off more smoke, if you combine them with dry logs, you can add a lot of flavor to your cook. They also burn so slowly that this combination can prolong the life of your fire bed.

If you combine green logs with dry, stack the dry logs on the bottom of the bed since they'll catch fire more quickly. Also, if you have a fire that's about to break down but you want to add another log to push the temperature, a drier log would be the best choice since it will burn more quickly.

SHAPES OF WOOD

Logs come in several shapes. You have what we call square logs, which look like building blocks. The sides are straight with perfect corners, and since they were cut from the middle of the trunk, they don't have any bark. It's super easy to build fires with these.

There are flat logs, which aren't as thick as square logs but still have straight lines, which makes them easier to stack. Unlike square logs, however, they will have a side lined with bark. If you're looking to add more smoke, the bark will help you do this.

Both square and flat logs have flat edges, which work well in building a fire because their clean lines keep the fire compressed under the logs. This helps the fire burn more efficiently.

Wedge-shaped logs take more finagling to build a tight fire bed. Jonny will stack them

Round log.

Flat log.

close together with flat edge to flat edge, which tamps down the flames so they instead come up over the side of the pile.

These also work well as guardian logs, which are the logs that go in the smoker close to the exchange. If you place the flat end toward the fire, the airflow will go up and over the log into the chamber.

WOOD BARK AND WHAT IT DOES

For our logs, we definitely use the bark on the wood (not to be confused with the bark that forms on the brisket as it cooks). We love it because this nubby shell on the log provides heaps of smoke, especially for shorter cooks, such as for turkey or ribs. In the beginning, we try to load the smoker with the barkiest logs because we want the meat to be hit with as much smoke as possible. And since we're only cooking with post oak, which is modestly flavored, we need as much smoke as possible.

Sure, you'll see the smoke coming out of the smokestack more, but in the beginning, this heavier smoke is just fine. It's flavor. For longer cooks, such as for briskets, we can get away with using only the logs that have less bark because it's going to end up smoky just by being in the smoker for 12 hours. But for turkeys and ribs, we'll choose the barkier logs to ensure that it tastes good.

There's been some talk about clean smoke being superior to so-called dirty smoke. Dirty smoke means that you can see a white and gray plume coming out of the smokestack, and clean smoke means you can't see anything at all. We have no problem with dirty, heavier smoke, especially at the beginning of your cook, since this is where the flavor will be found.

You will eventually want to start using less-barky logs as you go longer into the cook so your meat doesn't get too smoky, which can be off-putting to some. But don't freak out if you see black smoke coming out of the smokestack in the beginning. Or even if on hour 10 of a long brisket cook you suddenly have dirty smoke again, don't worry. Remember, dirty smoke is flavor. If you don't want your meat to taste like smoke, you might as well just cook it in an oven!

LIGHTING A FIRE

The goal of your first fire is to start building your coal bed. To begin, first clean out the firebox of all ashes and other debris from prior cooks. You always want the logs to be as low as possible, and junk in the box will prevent this.

We also position our logs closer to the firebox door, which helps keep the fire as far as possible from the meat. This is especially important when working with a backyard smoker.

After we've cleaned out the firebox, we start with charcoal, the kind that comes in a bag that you can find at the grocery store—nothing fancy. We like to put a small handful of the charcoal in the center of the box, then place two logs on either side.

Next, we'll stack two logs on top of the bottom two logs, crosswise. Now, if you're working with regular-size logs in a backyard smoker, you may have to angle the logs to get them to fit. You also could use a wood splitter and cut the logs in half, but we don't ever mess with that.

After we've built our bed, we then light it with a long lighter and let it go.

For the damper and the door, we recommend opening the damper all the way and leaving the door a quarter open. That way, there's plenty of airflow to get the fire going.

We let this first fire burn down until it forms a coal bed. We then break down the spent logs with a shovel. If there are any big chunks still ignited, just push those to the back of the chamber away from where you'll be stacking your new logs.

Leave the simmering coals close to the door to use in your new build. And now you have a coal bed that will form the foundation for the rest of your cook!

BUILDING FIRES

After you have your initial coal bed, it's time to build a new fire. Before each build, we use our shovel to break down the burnt logs, shifting any ignited chunks to the back of the firebox. We then smooth out the coal bed with the shovel to make a low, even layer. If it's late in the cook and you have lots of ashes, you can scoop out some of those, too, since they don't contribute anything but height, which we don't want.

We primarily use two styles of fire at Goldee's—a bundle fire and a log cabin fire. For the bundle fire, we aim to create an inefficient fire that produces lots of smoke. It's great for shorter cooks, such as turkey and ribs, where you want to get as much color and flavor as possible in a short amount of time. The log cabin fire is more efficient, and we use this for our longer cooks, like brisket and beef ribs.

To build a bundle fire, take the logs and start stacking them in the coal bed, all facing toward the cooking chamber. If you're working with flat logs or wedge-shaped logs, place the bark side down in the coal bed since that will produce more smoke. Just keep stacking the logs until you reach the temperature you need.

To build a log cabin fire, begin by smoothing out the coal bed into the center of the firebox. Next, take two logs and position each facing into the cooking chamber on the outside of the coal bed. The coal bed is now in between two logs.

Bundle fire.

For the second layer, stack two or three logs on top of the first layer in the opposite direction. For each layer you make, you will keep alternating directions in a crisscross style (much like how a log cabin is built, hence the name).

Remember, the goal is to keep the fire low. This is why for your first layer, in either style, you have the logs nestled into the coals (for a bundle fire) or positioned even with the coals (for a log cabin fire). This way, when the logs ignite, they will be physically lower in the box and the flames will be less likely to reach into the cooking chamber. Your second layer will also be closer to the coals, which will reduce airflow and keep the fire from going too crazy.

When building your wood layers, the closer the logs are together, the less airflow there will be between the logs, which will keep the fire lower. However, if you want the fire to be more efficient with taller flames, you can space the logs farther apart and the flames will rise in the space between logs.

If you have green logs, don't use them on the bottom layer. They will take too long to ignite. We use these on the second and third layers. That said, also try to avoid super-thin logs on the bottom layer. They ignite too quickly and also burn more quickly. The resulting spikes in temperature and tall flames will not only cause the meats to singe but will also create an environment where you're rebuilding fires more often. While not every log in your stack will be perfect, try to aim for thicker ones for long cooks such as briskets.

How you position your logs on your second and above layers also will play a role in the efficiency of your fire. For instance, the farther apart the logs are, the greater the airflow

Building a log cabin fire.

between the logs. This means you'll have flames shooting up in several spots, which can get wild.

When your logs are closer together, however, the flames will come up only over the sides of the stack. This fire will be more contained and less likely to go into the chamber. The logs will also tamp down the flames. When you add a log to a stack, if there is a flame below, the log will push it down and to the side since the log is now restricting airflow.

When building a fire, we put shorter logs in the middle so they won't affect the height of the row as much. The rear log and the front log are ideally the same height, which will make stacking the next layer easier.

Sometimes, your firebox may be too narrow to build a traditional log cabin shape with the wood positioned at 90 degrees. In this instance, once you have your coal bed, position your logs in a diagonal X shape for the bottom layer. Position this layer at an angle facing the firebox door opening, and place the logs for the second layer in the opposite direction.

HOW OFTEN TO PUT ON NEW LOGS AND REBUILD YOUR FIRES

There is no set guide for how often to rebuild your fires. Many factors come into play, such as the size of your firebox, the moisture content of your wood, your damper position, and whether your firebox is insulated. In time, you'll get a sense of how long each fire will typically last.

We recommend checking your first fire after about 30 minutes. You'll know it's time to build a new fire when the logs are disintegrating and easily shatter with a light touch of the shovel.

CONTROL: FIREBOX DOOR, DAMPER, SMOKER DOOR

In the beginning, we have the damper open. This increases the pull of the air through the chamber, which helps the logs burn more evenly but also gets the fire up to a good temp and builds a solid coal bed right off the bat.

Once we have our coal bed and begin building subsequent beds, we close the damper halfway, which traps heat in the chamber and will not only keep the beds burning more slowly but also cut time off of your cook. It also produces more smoke as well, which is what you want for flavor.

An open damper burns the logs so quickly that the airflow is too fast for cooking. Instead of caressing the meat, the air just rushes out of the smoke chamber. Also, the logs will burn too quickly and you won't get the full potential out of the wood. This is inefficient not only for the cook but also for your wallet since you'll be going through a lot more logs.

After we build and light the fire, we close the door almost all the way, leaving it open about an inch, which also traps more heat. The key to a pleasant, successful cook is an even fire that holds its temps. Now, if your temperature fluctuates a little bit, say 25 degrees in either direction from your target, don't worry about it.

Once we're in the cook, we make more adjustments for airflow with the door rather than the damper, as we feel that the damper has a stronger effect on the airflow and can cause larger spikes. If it spikes too high (or falls too low) then you have a problem. But small variations will sort themselves out. The key to all of this is to be chill and have fun. You have a tasty meal waiting for you at the end!

If you do have a huge spike upward, one trick we like is to open the chamber doors, which can drop the temperature quickly because so much air exits the smoker. After you open the doors, leave them open until the thermometer has moved to 25 degrees below your target, then close it.

With the airflow more contained, the temperature will soon rise to your target, and you'll be good to go! However, if your fire is too low to reach your target temperature, then you'll want to add more logs.

Goldee's
BAR-B-Q

PITMASTER PROFILE

JONNY WHITE

Jonny drives a truck. His full name is Jonny Ray White, and it would not be a surprise to learn a man with such a name would drive a Ford 4×4. That was the style of his first truck. After Goldee's became number one, however, Jonny traded in his Ford for a Honda. He also has long dropped being called Jonny Ray and now goes by either Jonny or Jirby, a name he coined as a portmanteau of *Jonny* and *Kirby*, the name of his favorite Nintendo character.

While all the Goldee's owners drive Hondas, only Jonny's is a truck. And while many Texans in trucks drive them because they are a symbol of Texas money, Jonny's truck gets used as it was intended. When he pulls up at Goldee's, he walks to the back of his truck and pulls out a box. Or maybe a stack of chairs. Perhaps it's buckets and fans to keep the line waiters cool in the late-July heat. No matter the day, Jonny is always bringing something to Goldee's to improve the experience for everyone.

Even when Jonny is simply sitting in silence, you can see his mind firing white hot. He's always coming up with a fresh idea and tapping into that excitement of creating something new, whether it's deciding to smoke the ribs with the damper open the entire cook or frying up balls of bread dough and then filling them with banana pudding.

"I would love to be a doughnut baker," said Jonny as he was preparing his new dessert creation for the apprentices. He then listed all the styles of doughnuts that would be on his menu and contemplated the carb-heavy yet delicious field research he'd have to undertake to come up with his ideal pastry. His eyes were glowing, and we hadn't seen him that happy in quite some time.

Jonny is one of the most talented pitmasters in the world, and he could spend the rest of his life resting on the glory of his sublime brisket. But he's created a new concept called Ribee's while still helping at Goldee's. He also loves to teach so the world can be filled with beautiful barbecue.

6 HOW THE SAUSA

GE GETS MADE

For more on cooking brisket, keep reading. For now, however, we're going to talk about sausage.

Jonny wanted to see if the restaurant could pull together and produce a large number of briskets—say, one hundred—and almost everyone was there that day. He made a plan to cook a hundred briskets and donate them to a local food pantry. When trimming that many briskets in one sitting, you're going to be left with lots of leftover trim.

One of our regular by-products from cooking briskets is lots of decent beef. Making sausage with these cuts is the ideal solution since it uses up all the meat and fat but also gives us a place to explore new flavors. Sausage can be fun.

That day, Lane tasked Nupohn with preparing all the brisket trim for sausage. Nupohn set up a station with cutting boards, meat, and seasonings, then began the process. It starts with cutting the beef down into usable pieces, trimming off the elements you don't want in sausage, such as soft fat and silver skin, and then coating the chopped meat in salt, cure, pepper, and spices.

Sausage making for us is a three-day process. On the first day, we trim and season the meat. On the second day, we mix the sausage paste and stuff it into casings. On the third day, we cold smoke the links.

Sure, people come to us for our succulent brisket, but preparing sausage is one of our favorite activities since we have so much leeway in what we can create. While our brisket, ribs, and turkey all use a combination of the same flavors that come from salt, pepper, and our house seasoned salt, sausage can be made into an infinite variety of flavor profiles. It's so much fun!

These days at the restaurant, we stick to our two core sausages—one with our house blend of salt, pepper, and garlic, and our jalapeño cheese sausage. Occasionally, we'll offer specials such as our Lao Texas sausage and beerwurst.

When we first opened and weren't busy, we played around and threw a multitude of different ingredients into our sausage mix. Every week there was a new sausage on the menu, and if you missed it, you would probably never get to try it again.

This wasn't because we weren't satisfied with what we produced; it was just that we had so many ideas we were excited to try that we kept coming up with new links. This is the joy of making sausage—the possibilities are endless.

In this book, we give you four recipes, which are a solid foundation to begin making sausage at home. But first, let's talk about our recipe philosophy. If you understand why we combine the ingredients the way we do, it will bring depth to your own sausage making. In time, you will be able to come up with your own combinations.

At Goldee's, we primarily make beef sausage. Barbecue restaurants do this as a means of using up their meat trim. We use our pork rib trim in our Kennedale pork hash (page 212), which leaves us with an abundance of brisket trim. This is why our sausages are beef.

That said, Jalen will be quick to tell you that pork sausages not only can be juicier but are also easier to make. As we go into more details about our recipe philosophy, know that since you probably won't have hundreds of pounds of brisket trim to use, you can make any of our recipes with pork butt too.

Now, let's get back to the essence of sausage, which is an emulsion of meat, fat, and liquid. If you're not familiar with the term *emulsion*, it's the suspension of two or more ingredients into a smooth blend.

Have you ever made an oil and vinegar dressing? When you pour the two ingredients into a jar, for instance, you'll see that they don't naturally combine but instead layer on top of each other. To get them to form an emulsion, you need to vigorously whisk the two until their molecular structures yield and the two merge into one. Or something like that. We're not very clear on the scientific terminology.

Making sausage is similar. We want the meat and fat to meld into a cohesive form. Think about a hamburger. It's also a blend of fat and meat, but it's crumbly and coarse. This is because when you form the patties, there's nothing there to combine the two into one, hence the rough texture.

On the other hand, if you're making meatballs, you are likely adding eggs, liquid, and starch to the blend of meat and fat. As you work these ingredients together, all the elements start to bind. And most meatballs are much smoother than a hamburger.

It's this same philosophy that goes into making sausage. All the ingredients we include are there to bind everything into one tasty package.

SAUSAGE INGREDIENTS

Now let's get into more detail about what we put into each batch.

MEAT AND FAT

At Goldee's, we use brisket trim and hard beef fat, which comes from the deckle on the back side of the brisket. Sometimes we'll incorporate our pork rib and pork belly trims into our brisket blend if we need to stretch it further.

As for the fat, with brisket sausage we use hard fat because it's easier to work with. Soft fat can smear in the grinder, though if it's all you have, you can use it. What's the difference? Well, the hard fat on a brisket is a plate of dense fat found on the underside. It's denser than the fat that marbles through the meat, and this structure makes it less likely to overheat.

When grinding the meat with the fat, all the action in the grinder produces heat energy, which can cause structural issues in your final product if the fat gets too warm. We'll go into more ways to prevent that later when we discuss how to make sausage, but if you have hard fat, we recommend using it since it's less likely to melt.

If you want to make a pork sausage, you can take our recipes and use pork butt. The wonder of pork butt is that it naturally has the perfect meat-to-fat ratio, so you can take a roast and use it immediately without having to weigh the meat and fat. You also don't have to worry about finding hard fat to combine with the meat, since the perfect amount of fat is already there.

We love making sausage with only pork. It's just not feasible for us at the restaurant since we have hundreds of pounds of beef trim that we need to use instead. However, if you're new to making sausage, starting with a pork butt may be something to consider.

SALT

Salt is a vital ingredient because it brings all the flavors together. Without salt, your sausage will be sorely lacking in taste. We use table salt, as it's easiest to work with and its fine grains distribute the salty flavor throughout the entire sausage.

This salt has some preserving powers. But because the meat stays at a temperature that's in the danger zone of below 140°F for several hours while it's cold smoking, we also add curing salt to our blend.

There are two pink curing salts. One is Prague powder number one and the other is Prague powder number two. For our sausages, we use number one. What's the difference? Well, number one is a blend of salt and nitrites, and number two also has nitrates added to this blend.

For our purposes, we need only the nitrites and not the nitrates found in number two. The latter is used for meats that aren't going to be cooked. However, we still want the curing salt because it keeps the sausage safe while we cold smoke it. The sausage will be kept under a safe temperature for hours, and the cure prevents any toxins from forming. It also gives the sausage a more vibrant color.

You want to be careful, though. The salt is pink, and to the untrained eye it may resemble Himalayan pink salt, which is a rock salt found in Pakistan. It is a table and cooking salt, not a curing salt. We have a friend who made this mistake when she was in culinary school. She was preparing a dish that required quite a bit of salt. She decided to use Himalayan pink salt.

However, when going through her pantry, she grabbed the wrong pink salt. After adding handfuls of curing salt to her dish, it was inedible. Her instructor was horrified. Also, know that too much pink curing salt can cause a dish to turn toxic. We keep our levels at a minimum, but we just wanted to share this cautionary tale with you. Too much curing salt is bad news.

SPICES AND FRESH VEGETABLES

Black pepper is our main flavoring besides salt. We use coarse ground, 16-mesh black pepper at the restaurant, and that's what we recommend you use too.

For spices, our favorites to use are garlic powder, onion powder, and pepper. You need to be careful with some spices, such as paprika and dried chilies, since they're acidic and can break up your sausage.

You could easily stop with the spices, but we also like to throw some fresh vegetables into our sausage. Garlic is a favorite addition, and we use fresh jalapeños too. Green onions are fun, and fresh herbs will also give the blends pungency.

When adding spices and fresh vegetables, however, you want to be cautious about acidity. For instance, dried red chilies are acidic, as are citrus fruits like lime, fresh onions, and tomatoes (or tomato paste). If there are too many acidic ingredients, the sausage will break and be coarse. By broken, we mean the sausage will be crumbly and dry. It won't form that smooth emulsion we've been telling you about. Garlic and fresh herbs are fine, though.

The paste formed when mixing all the ingredients is a balanced blend of meat, fat, liquid, and spices. Like an emulsion such as vinaigrette or mayonnaise, these ingredients are held together in a suspension, and too much acidity will tear this balance apart.

Now, please don't ask us to get too technical about the science behind this, but we know from years of experience!

LIQUID

Stock is a great addition to sausage because it has the best flavor. At the restaurant, though, we use water, and it also works. You also can use beer, though we prefer lighter lagers over dark beers. We'd be careful with acidic liquids such as lime and lemon juice, as they'll break up the sausage.

MILK POWDER

This is what binds the sausage together and keeps it from being grainy. There are other binders, but this is our favorite. It also helps the sausage retain moisture. You want to use low-fat milk powder so you don't increase the fat ratio. Most of the milk powder you find at the grocery store is low-fat, so it's not hard to find.

SAUSAGE RATIOS

A lot of our recipes follow a bare-bones formula. All our fat ratios are the same, and all our meat ratios are the same. Our salt ratio is the same, as are our liquid and milk powder ratios. Once you get the hang of the ratios and formula, you can play around and put pretty much anything you want into your sausages.

We begin by figuring out our meat-to-fat ratio. The range we go with is 70 percent meat to 30 percent fat up to 75 percent meat to 25 percent fat.

Too much fat makes the sausage greasy, and the goal is to have a good mouthfeel. But anything less than 25 percent fat will be dry and crumbly. This 25 to 30 percent range of fat is our sweet spot for that perfect juicy link.

For the salt, we use 0.2 percent of the total weight. This is the sweet spot we've found for the optimum amount of saltiness.

We also add curing salt at a ratio of 0.2 ounces per 5 pounds of meat. Because we're cold smoking, the cure keeps the meat from going bad as it cooks, and it also helps give the sausage a more vibrant color.

Most of our spices can be done to taste, though we have a ratio for black pepper, which is 2 percent of the total weight. For our specific blends, we also add garlic and onion powder at 1 percent of the total weight.

When you add fresh vegetables such as jalapeños to the sausage, you'll want to salt these a bit. This keeps the salt ratio throughout the sausage at an optimum level.

RATIOS FOR KEY SAUSAGE INGREDIENTS

MEAT TO FAT: 70/30 percent; MEAT TO FAT: 75/25 percent

SALT: 2 percent total meat weight

CURING SALT, PRAGUE POWDER NUMBER ONE: 0.2 percent total weight

PEPPER: 2 percent total meat weight

GARLIC AND ONION POWDER: 1 percent total meat weight (each)

MILK POWDER: 4 percent total meat weight

LIQUID: 10 percent total meat weight

VEGETABLES: Add salt equal to 1 percent total vegetable weight

If you use fresh vegetables, they will add extra liquid. We suggest looking up the average amount of liquid per vegetable and then factoring this into your liquid ratio. For instance, our jalapeño cheese sausage was coming out too wet and we couldn't figure out why, but then we realized it was from the peppers.

To do this takes a lot of math, but it's worth it. When we realized the fresh peppers were causing too much liquid in our jalapeño cheese links, we looked up the amount of liquid and then subtracted that from the total amount of liquid we were adding. That gave us the ideal ratio of liquid to meat.

The same goes if you're adding an ingredient that has added salt, such as cheese. You'll look up how much salt is in the ingredient and then subtract that amount from your total salt amount.

SAUSAGE-MAKING PROCESS

Once you have your recipe and ingredients in place, the fun begins! As we said, our sausage making is a three-day process. While none of the steps are terribly challenging (though some will say that forming links is the toughest part of the job), they do take time and a methodical nature. None of the steps can be done out of order, and it's important to be very precise in your recipe. Otherwise, the ratios of ingredients may not form a juicy, tight, and succulent link.

Of course, there's also lots of special equipment required. We assume you have a smoker, which is why you're holding this book—though, surprisingly, that's not the key tool. In fact, all these sausages taste just as good cooked in the oven without going through the cold smoke. Of course, smoke is a key flavor, but it's not the most important tool.

Instead, you do need a scale, a grinder, and a sausage stuffer to make these recipes. Like many of you, we used to work in volume measurements that called for a teaspoon of that and a tablespoon of this. While we still may work in volume for some of our kitchen recipes, with sausage we've now switched to weight for precise and consistent results.

For production, you may have a meat grinder and sausage-stuffing attachment for your stand mixer. If you want to try making sausage once, give these a try.

However, we highly recommend sourcing a dedicated grinder and stuffer. Ask around—perhaps you have a friend who makes sausage. Or maybe your library has an objects collection and they include a grinder or a stuffer. You can even get lower-priced entry-level versions. All we're saying is this: If you want to use the stand mixer, go ahead, but it doesn't come close to the ease and fun that making sausage can be.

With all that in mind, let's get started.

DAY 1

TRIMMING

While we make beef sausage at the restaurant, Jalen prefers pork sausage, as he feels it binds better and has a smoother texture. Beef can be trickier to work with. If you're new to making sausage, you may want to begin with pork.

BRISKET

We start with our brisket trim. The best part of the brisket to use is the long cut that you make down the sides (see brisket trimming, pages 126–131), as it's mainly lean and it's easy to cut off the fat. You can use the mohawk (see page 128 for more about this cut), but it's trickier to come up with the exact meat-to-fat ratio since it's more marbled.

Your goal is to trim off as much of the soft fat and silver skin from any trim you have so you can get an accurate ratio and prevent the fat and silver skin from getting stuck in the grinder plate. You can use a 10-inch chef's knife for trimming, or you can use a boning knife—whichever you feel is most comfortable.

After trimming the meat, weigh what you have so you can determine the appropriate ratio of hard fat.

The hard fat comes from the back side of the brisket on the deckle. If there's meat on it, trim it from the fat. You can add that meat to your meat ratio if you like. If you don't have enough deckle hard fat, we recommend using the fat from the mohawk, as it's more solid than the top fat.

Cut the meat into 1-inch cubes.

PORK

We recommend using a bone-in pork butt, as it's less expensive. But you can use a boneless one too. While it costs more, it's easier to work with.

If using a bone-in pork butt, find the bone with your hands (it will be sticking out on the end) and then follow the bone with your knife to remove it. Trim any meat off the bone and then toss the bone or save it for pork stock (see page 201).

All pork butts have a lymph node gland. It tastes pretty funky, so you want to remove it. While boneless pork butts might have had the gland removed, it will always be in a bone-in pork butt that you trim.

To find the gland, after you remove the bone, butterfly the butt in half like you're opening a book and the gland will be at the center of the butt where the bone was. It looks like a knobby, bubbly piece of organ and fat. Sometimes it will have a green tint or be a darker red than the meat. When you find it, just trim it away from the meat and toss it.

After you've removed the bone and gland, cut the meat into 1-inch cubes. You don't need to trim the rest of the fat away since the butt already has the perfect ratio of fat to meat.

SEASONING

After trimming and cubing the meat, we then season it and refrigerate it overnight in a covered container. We do this because it lets the salt and spices penetrate the meat, and it will have a better flavor.

To season, toss the cubed meats with the seasonings you're going to use. Mix it until all the spices are sticking to the meat. As the meat rests overnight, the seasonings will adhere even more.

Seasoning the meat.

CASINGS

At the restaurant, we use all-pork casings that are 28 to 30 millimeters, which is a standard size. Sausage casings are classified by their diameter, which is typically measured in millimeters. If you don't eat pork, you can use lamb casings, which run a bit smaller and are more delicate.

To prepare the casings, on the first day we rinse the casings in warm water. The casings arrive packed in salt, and you want to dissolve that out. The warm water helps with this process. You can rinse at your sink, getting the water on both the outside and the inside of the casings by positioning the end of the casing on the faucet and letting the water run through it like a balloon.

After the rinse, we soak them overnight. We fill a quart-size container with water, stir in baking soda, place the casings in the prepared water, and then refrigerate overnight.

The second day is the busiest. We'll be grinding, mixing, and stuffing the sausages. It's now time to get some rest!

GRINDING

Before grinding the meat, make sure it's super cold. Two hours before grinding, put the beef in the freezer. Its ideal grinding temperature is 32 to 34°F. Pork can go into the freezer for 1½ hours before grinding since it doesn't need to be as cold. It can be ground at 38°F.

We use a three-eighths plate die on our grinder. The most important thing is to make sure everything is cold. It's at this stage we'll add fresh vegetables, such as garlic. You could add jalapeños at this point too, though they release so much moisture through the grinder that we prefer to dice and salt them separately and stir them into the ground sausage blend later in the process.

Grind everything together—the meat, hard fat, and vegetables. We pack the grinder's feed tube with a handful of pork, some of the hard fat, and then vegetables, repeating this layering as we grind.

When grinding, you want to go slow. Let the motor do the work of pulling the meat through the grinder, and don't try to force it through with the damper. If it does get stuck, use a gentle push to get it going again.

Because we're using such a small die on the grinder, we only grind once. Some people do a double grind, but that affects the texture if the meat isn't chilled between grinds—the meat will become warm and start to smear.

Grinding the meat.

One way to combat that is to add ice to the grinder, but at the restaurant, we don't have an ice maker so we've made it work by doing only one grind with a small plate.

MIXING

This is when you add your liquid, your cheese, and your milk powder to the ground meat.

Again, make sure that everything is cold. You can use your stand mixer, or you can do it by hand. Add the ingredients to your mixer and then mix for about 5 minutes or until it's all come together and you can see little fat strands as fine as hair start to form.

Our very scientific test is to take a small handful of the mix, pat it into your hand, and then turn your hand over. If it sticks to your hand, then it's ready. If it's not, then keep mixing.

It's at this point you'll know whether your sausage is broken. If after 15 minutes, the sausage mix hasn't passed the hand test and you don't see the thin fat strands, then it's likely that something went wrong in the process.

Mixing the ground meat.

Perhaps the meat was too warm when being ground, there's not enough fat, there's not enough liquid, or there's too much acid in the blend.

To fix this, you can freeze what you do have for a couple of hours before trying to mix again. If you're certain all your ingredients were super chilled before going through the grinder, you also can try adding more fat and/or cold water before mixing again.

After the sausage mix has become sticky and come together, it's wise to fry up a small test patty to see if you like the seasonings. Heat a skillet on medium, add a teaspoon of oil, and then fry the meat for 5 to 7 minutes, turning once, or until it's browned.

Take a bite and see how it tastes. If you're pleased, then continue to stuff. If not, make any adjustments you want.

CASINGS

Take the casings out of the refrigerator. Dump out the water and then rinse the casings one more time in warm water. Now they're ready to use!

Any unrinsed casings that you don't use can be kept in the refrigerator for a year. Just leave them packed in salt. For the already-rinsed casings, you can dry them off, pack them in salt, and then top them with water until ready to use again.

STUFFING

We use an LEM 25-pound stuffer, though they go down to a 5-pound stuffer. Haka is a good brand, or any brand made in Germany will be good too.

To start, we clamp the stuffer down on the table. This keeps the stuffer from moving.

You'll see that the stuffer has three parts—the hopper, which is the rectangular reservoir where you place the meat; the crank, which you turn to push the meat through; and the horn, which is where you place the casing and where the meat comes through.

To start, pack the meat into the hopper. You want it to be compact and you don't want any air bubbles, so press it down with your hands. If any air bubbles come through and end up in the sausage, these pockets will fill up with grease as the sausage cooks, and when you bite into the sausage, you'll get a mouthful of grease that hurts.

Now get your rinsed casings, find the end, and then slide it onto the horn. Leave about an inch hanging off the end of the horn. Before tying off the end, turn the crank until you see just a small smidge of the sausage coming through the horn. This releases any pent-up air and pressure. Now tie off the end. It's time to continue stuffing!

For technique, we wet our nondominant hand (so if you're right-handed, you'll use your left hand), then gently hold the casing. We apply a little bit of pressure, but mainly the hand is there to support and guide the casing as it gets filled and moves along.

We use our dominant hand to turn the crank, which forces the meat through the horn. Try to go at an even pace so you don't lose control of the sausage as it stuffs. It takes some practice to find your rhythm, but you'll get there.

Be aware that when you let go of the crank, it will start spinning back toward you. Be careful not to get bopped in the head by a runaway crank. It's happened to all of us!

If the casing breaks as you're stuffing, stop the crank. With a knife, cut off the casing where the break happened and then start the process over again.

After you've stuffed the casing, it's time to form links.

We make ours about 6 inches wide, or as Jalen says, the width of his hand. Start at the end that's already tied off, and then pinch 6 inches away on the casing, where you want to make a tie to form the first link.

While you're pinching the casing with one hand, with your other hand rotate the link away from you for several rotations until the knot on the casing is secure.

Start with about three or four rotations and see how that holds. If you do too many

Tying off the end of the casing on the horn before stuffing.

Stuffing the sausage.

Tying the links.

rotations, the link may pop, and if you do too few, it might not stay tied. It's hard to say an exact right number because the amount of pressure each link has is dependent on how you stuffed the casing. So, three or four turns is a good way to begin.

For the next length, about 6 inches away from the previous tie, pinch the casing then rotate it toward you, in the opposite direction from the prior spin. Do this several times as well.

Keep working down the length of the sausage, alternating the rotation direction for each tie, until you're done.

As you move along, you'll get a feel for your technique. The tighter the sausages are, the better they're going to be after cooking, but if they're too tight, the casings will pop. It's a balance that you'll figure out over time.

If the casing does become too tight and pops, that's okay! As Jalen says, not a day goes by that he doesn't pop at least one casing, so know that it's a common occurrence.

When this happens, just cut off the popped link and then tie a knot on the new end of the sausage strand. From there, continue forming links down what's left of the strand. For the popped link, you can remove the meat from the casing and put the meat back in the hopper to be stuffed again.

You'll want to throw out the popped casing because it's useless. However, if you're competitive like us, you could hold on to your burst casings and when you're done, compare stacks with the others on your team to see who popped the most. If you make a game of it, y'all might not feel so annoyed when it happens. And trust us, it will!

After tying off the links, we rest the sausage intact overnight before cutting. This way, they have a chance to dry and they won't unravel on you. To cut the casings, use a sharp knife and cut in the center of the knot. While we cut ours into links before cold smoking, you can smoke the entire casing and cut them after they're done if you prefer.

COLD SMOKE

Because the principles of cold smoking sausage apply to anything you wish to cold smoke, we've included that method in chapter 7 on page 183.

If, however, you don't have a smoker, you can certainly finish these sausages at home. You can cook them either in the oven or on the stovetop. We recommend lightly greasing a skillet and cooking them in the oven at 375°F until darkened and sizzling and at an internal temperature of 160°F, about 20 to 25 minutes.

Alternatively, you can cook the unsmoked sausages on the stovetop. To do this, place them in a skillet, add enough water to the skillet to reach halfway up the sausages, and then cook on medium heat until the water is evaporated and the sausages are darkened and sizzling, with an internal temperature of 160°F, about 10 to 15 minutes.

SAUSAGE RECIPES

We're always messing around with new sausage ideas. It's this flexibility in flavorings that makes it one of the most satisfying things to prepare. Sure, there are times that our experiments don't work out for us, but it's still fun to create new things and explore an infinite number of possibilities.

Here you will find four of our favorite sausage recipes. Each one showcases a different skill, such as working with fresh vegetables and cheese, as in our jalapeño cheese sausage; mixing with beer, as in our beerwurst; using unusual spices, as in our Lao Texas sausage, or creating a classic Central Texas style link, as in our house sausage.

Our dream is for you to work with our recipes and then use them as a springboard to craft your own sausage creations that reflect what you enjoy and love.

HOUSE SAUSAGE

This is our original sausage that we always offer on the menu. It's a standard Central Texas link flavored with salt, pepper, and garlic. The meat's grind is fine, which creates a smoother texture. And it's not too spicy and has a deep smoky and savory flavor with plenty of juice and snap.

SAUSAGE INGREDIENTS

3¾ pounds (1.7 kilograms) brisket trim
2½ tablespoons table salt
1 teaspoon number one pink curing salt
2 tablespoons coarse black pepper
2 tablespoons mustard seeds
1½ tablespoons garlic powder
1½ tablespoons onion powder
10 cloves fresh garlic
1½ pounds (680 grams) hard brisket fat
¾ cup (188 milliliters) low-fat milk powder
1½ cups (125 milliliters) water or stock
Safflower oil, for frying

CASING INGREDIENTS

28-millimeter natural pork casing
1½ teaspoons baking soda

SPECIAL EQUIPMENT

Metal mixing bowls
Meat grinder
Stand mixer
Sharp knife
Sausage stuffer

TRIM MEAT

Trim the brisket of any silver skin and discard. Cube the trimmed meat into 1-inch pieces. Place the cubed meat into a nonreactive food-safe container, such as a wide mixing bowl.

SEASON MEAT

Stir together the table salt, curing salt, black pepper, mustard seeds, garlic powder, and onion powder until well blended.

Pour the spice blend over the cubed meat, then use your hands to toss the meat with the spices until all pieces are well coated. If any spices fall to the bottom of the container, continue to toss until the spices are adhering.

OVERNIGHT REST

Cover the meat and refrigerate it overnight.

RINSE CASINGS

At the sink, rinse the casings in warm water until any visible salt has been removed. Fill a quart-size container with warm water and the baking soda.

Stir until the soda is combined, then place the rinsed casings in the water. Let them sit in the water overnight.

DAY 2

GRINDING

For this step, you'll be using your grinder. You will also need another mixing bowl or sheet pan to place at the base of the grinder.

Before grinding, toss the meat with any seasonings that may have fallen to the bottom of the container, then place the seasoned meat in the freezer.

Cube the hard fat into 1-inch pieces, and place it in the freezer with the meat.

Also place in the freezer the metal parts of the grinder, which include the grinder plate, the blade, the hopper, the augur, and the cover. Keep everything in the freezer for 30 minutes so they can become cold.

While everything chills, set up your grinder and your station. Place a mixing bowl or sheet pan at the base of the grinder to receive the ground meat.

Gather your garlic cloves.

After 30 minutes, remove the grinder parts from the freezer and assemble your grinder.

Remove the meat from the freezer and begin grinding. You want to go slowly so the meat doesn't overheat. Working in batches, fill the hopper with several cubes of the meat, a couple of garlic cloves, and a couple of the fat cubes, in that order.

Turn on the grinder and let the grinder pull the meat through. If you need to tamp it down, do it gently, and don't force the meat through the grinder. Let the motor (or the crank) do the heavy work.

Continue to feed the meat, garlic, and fat into the hopper until all of it has been ground.

MIXING THE SAUSAGE PASTE

Place the ground meat in the freezer. If you're using a stand mixer, place the mixer's mixing bowl and flat beater in the freezer with the meat so they can also chill. If you'll be using your hands, place a clean mixing bowl in the freezer. Place the liquid you'll be using in the freezer too.

Allow everything to chill for 30 minutes.

After 30 minutes, remove everything from the freezer. Place the ground meat into the mixing bowl. Add the milk powder and the chilled liquid. If using a stand mixer, attach the flat beater and beat on medium-low speed until a thick and sticky paste is formed, about 5 minutes.

If using your hands, blend the mixture with your hands until a sticky, well-blended paste is formed, about 10 minutes.

To test whether it's ready, take a small handful of the mixed sausage paste and pat it flat into your palm. Turn your palm over—if the meat adheres to your hand, it's ready for stuffing. If it slips off, however, keep grinding.

TASTE TEST

After mixing and before stuffing, you can do a taste test to see if the seasonings are to your liking.

Heat up a skillet on medium and add a teaspoon of safflower oil. Take a tablespoon-size portion of the mixed sausage paste and form it into a patty. Cook the test patty for 5 to 7 minutes, turning once, or until it's browned and beginning to crisp.

Taste the patty. If you feel the sausage needs any seasoning adjustments, add these to the mixer with the sausage paste and then mix until well blended.

Repeat as desired.

Once you're happy with the sausage paste, place

it in the freezer while you set up your casings and stuffing station.

CASING PREP BEFORE STUFFING

Remove the soaked casings from the refrigerator. Dump out the water, then rinse the casings at the sink in warm water.

Fill a clean container with warm water, and place the casings in there until you are ready to use them.

STUFFING

Assemble your stuffer.

If using a vertical dedicated stuffer, remove the sausage paste from the freezer and fill the hopper with the meat. Clamp down the piston so the air bubbles can escape.

If using a stand mixer or grinder with a stuffing attachment, fill the feed tube with the amount it will hold, pressing down to remove any air bubbles.

Take a 3-foot portion of casing (if your casings are longer, you can cut off a portion with a sharp knife). Wet the horn and then slide on all of the casing (for more detail, see page 99). Gently pull an inch of the casing off the end of the horn.

Press the meat through the hopper until you see a small bit of meat exit through the horn into the casing. Tie off the end, then proceed with stuffing the casing. (For more details and troubleshooting, see page 98.)

Once the casing is stuffed, repeat for the remainder of the sausage paste.

Form links down the length of the casing (see pages 98–100). After you form the links, with a sharp knife cut off the individual links, then place the sausages on a sheet pan. Allow to rest uncovered overnight in the refrigerator.

Any unused casings can be dried, repacked in salt, covered with water, and refrigerated until you are ready to use them. They should keep for a year, but check what your package recommends.

Set up your smoker for cold smoking (see page 183).

Cold smoke the links and then reheat before serving.

YIELD: 5 POUNDS SAUSAGE

HOUSE SAUSAGE, SHORT VERSION

Cube the meat, then combine with the table salt, curing salt, black pepper, mustard seeds, garlic powder, and onion powder until well blended. Refrigerate overnight.

Soak the casings overnight.

The second day, cube the hard fat. Chill in the freezer for 30 minutes with the seasoned meat.

Remove the seasoned meat from the freezer and grind the meat with the garlic cloves and cubed fat. Place the ground meat in the freezer again for 30 minutes.

After chilling, remove the ground meat from the freezer. Mix the ground meat, cheese, jalapeños, milk powder, and liquid until a sticky paste is formed.

Stuff the sausage paste into the casing. Form into links, then cut the individual links. Rest the sausage overnight uncovered in the refrigerator.

The third day, prepare your smoker for cold smoking. Cold smoke the sausages and then reheat before serving (see page 183).

JALAPEÑO CHEESE SAUSAGE

Some say that Texas smoked sausages with jalapeños were introduced at Louis Mueller Barbecue in Taylor. While we don't know whether this is true, we're grateful for whoever had the genius idea to combine Texas's state chili pepper with beef, spices, and smoke. Cubes of melted cheese only add to the richness and piquancy of this rich and juicy link.

3¾ pounds (1.7 kilograms) brisket trim
2½ tablespoons table salt
1 teaspoon number one pink curing salt
2 tablespoons coarse black pepper
1¼ pounds (567 grams) hard brisket fat
12 ounces (340 grams) cheddar cheese
15 whole jalapeños, seeded, diced, and salted
¾ cup (188 milliliters) milk powder
1 cup (250 milliliters) water
Safflower oil, for frying

CASING INGREDIENTS

28-millimeter natural pork casing
1½ teaspoons baking soda

SPECIAL EQUIPMENT

Metal mixing bowls
Meat grinder
Stand mixer
Sharp knife
Sausage stuffer
Sheet pans

DAY 1

TRIM MEAT

Trim the brisket of any silver skin and discard. Cube the trimmed meat into 1-inch pieces. Place the cubed meat into a nonreactive food-safe container, such as a wide mixing bowl.

SEASON MEAT

Stir together the table salt, curing salt, and black pepper until well blended.

Pour the spice blend over the cubed meat, then use your hands to toss the meat with the spices until all pieces are well coated. If any spices fall to the bottom of the container, continue to toss until the spices are adhering.

OVERNIGHT REST

Cover the meat and refrigerate it overnight.

RINSE CASINGS

At the sink, rinse the casings in warm water until any visible salt has been removed. Fill a quart-size container with warm water and the baking soda.

Stir until the soda is combined, then place the rinsed casings in the water. Let them sit in the water overnight.

DAY 2

GRINDING

For this step, you'll be using your grinder. You will also need another mixing bowl or sheet pan to place at the base of the grinder.

Before grinding, toss the meat with any seasonings that may have fallen to the bottom of the container, then place the seasoned meat in the freezer.

Cube the hard fat into 1-inch pieces, and place it in the freezer with the meat.

Also place in the freezer the metal parts of the grinder, which include the grinder plate, the blade, the hopper, the augur, and the cover. Keep everything in the freezer for 30 minutes so they can become cold.

While everything chills, set up your grinder and your station. Place a mixing bowl or sheet pan at the base of the grinder to receive the ground meat.

After 30 minutes, remove the grinder parts from the freezer and assemble your grinder.

Remove the meat from the freezer and begin grinding. You want to go slowly so the meat doesn't overheat. Working in batches, fill the hopper with several cubes of the meat and a couple of the fat cubes, in that order.

Turn on the grinder and let the grinder pull the meat through. If you need to tamp it down, do it gently, and don't force the meat through the grinder. Let the motor (or the crank) do the heavy work.

Continue to feed the meat and fat into the hopper until all of it has been ground.

MIXING THE SAUSAGE PASTE

Place the ground meat in the freezer. If you're using a stand mixer, place the mixer's mixing bowl and flat beater in the freezer with the meat so they can also chill. If you'll be using your hands, place a clean mixing bowl in the freezer. Place the liquid you'll be using in the freezer too.

Allow everything to chill for 30 minutes.

Meanwhile, cut the cheddar cheese into 1⁄4-inch cubes. Stem and seed the jalapeños, and finely dice.

After 30 minutes, remove everything from the freezer. Place the ground meat, cheese, and jalapeños into the mixing bowl. Add the milk powder and the chilled liquid. If using a stand mixer, attach the flat beater and beat on medium-low speed until a thick and sticky paste is formed, about 5 minutes.

If using your hands, blend the mixture with your hands until a sticky, well-blended paste is formed, about 10 minutes.

To test whether it's ready, take a small handful of the mixed sausage paste and pat it flat into your palm. Turn your palm over—if the meat adheres to your hand, it's ready for stuffing. If it slips off, however, keep grinding.

TASTE TEST

After mixing and before stuffing, you can do a taste test to see if the seasonings are to your liking.

Heat up a skillet on medium and add a teaspoon of safflower oil. Take a tablespoon-size portion of the mixed sausage paste and form it into a patty. Cook the test patty for 5 to 7 minutes, turning once, or until it's browned and beginning to crisp.

Taste the patty. If you feel the sausage needs any seasoning adjustments, add these to the mixer with the sausage paste and then mix until well blended.

Repeat as desired.

Once you're happy with the sausage paste, place it in the freezer while you set up your casings and stuffing station.

CASING PREP BEFORE STUFFING

Remove the soaked casings from the refrigerator. Dump out the water, then rinse the casings at the sink in warm water.

Fill a clean container with warm water, and place the casings in there until you are ready to use them.

STUFFING

Assemble your stuffer.

If using a vertical dedicated stuffer, remove the sausage paste from the freezer and fill the hopper with the meat. Clamp down the piston so the air bubbles can escape.

If using a stand mixer or grinder with a stuffing attachment, fill the feed tube with the amount it will hold, pressing down to remove any air bubbles.

Take a 3-foot portion of casing (if your casings are longer, you can cut off a portion with a sharp knife). Wet the horn and then slide on all the casing (for more detail, see page 99). Gently pull an inch of the casing off the end of the horn.

Press the meat through the hopper until you see a small bit of meat exit through the horn into the casing. Tie off the end, then proceed with stuffing the casing. (For more details and troubleshooting, see page 98.)

Once the casing is stuffed, repeat for the remainder of the sausage paste.

Form links down the length of the casing (see pages 98–100). After you form the links, with a sharp knife cut off the individual links, then place the sausages on a sheet pan. Allow to rest uncovered overnight in the refrigerator.

Any unused casings can be dried, repacked in salt, covered with water, and refrigerated until you are ready to use them. They should keep for a year, but check what your package recommends.

Set up your smoker for cold smoking (see page 183).

Cold smoke the links and then reheat before serving.

YIELD: 6 POUNDS SAUSAGE

JALAPEÑO CHEESE SAUSAGE, SHORT VERSION

Cube the meat, then combine with the table salt, curing salt, and black pepper until well blended. Refrigerate overnight.

Soak the casings overnight.

The second day, cube the hard fat. Chill the seasoned meat in the freezer for 30 minutes.

Remove the seasoned meat from the freezer, and grind the meat with the cubed fat. Place the ground meat in the freezer again for 30 minutes.

Cut cheese and jalapeños into ¼-inch pieces.

After chilling, remove the ground meat from the freezer. Mix with the cheese, jalapeños, milk powder, and liquid until a sticky paste is formed.

Stuff the sausage pastes into casings. Form into links, then cut the individual links. Rest the sausage overnight uncovered in the refrigerator.

The third day, prepare your smoker for cold smoking. Cold smoke the sausages and then reheat before serving (see page 183).

LAO TEXAS SAUSAGE

When we first moved back to DFW from Austin, we began exploring the area's vast Laotian scene with Nupohn, who is from Laos. He'd take us to his favorite restaurants, and one of the standard items on the menu is Laotian sausage.

Typically, it's fresh pork sausage. But we thought we could give it a Texas barbecue twist and take the ingredients, such as lemongrass, lime, shallots, garlic, and chilies, and slowly cure it and smoke it instead.

In the beginning, we made it with all fresh vegetables, but once we discovered that almost all the ingredients are also available in ground form, we switched our recipe. Using ground spices ensures more accuracy.

Here's the recipe, which can be prepared with either pork butt, which is traditional, or beef, which we do at the restaurant. To serve, we offer sticky rice (page 211) and a garlic cilantro dipping sauce called jeow som (page 197). These are the standard Laotian add-ons, but this bright and lively sausage stands on its own too.

SAUSAGE INGREDIENTS

4½ pounds (2.04 kilograms) pork butt (or beef)
5½ tablespoons table salt
1½ teaspoons number one pink curing salt
1½ tablespoons black pepper
½ pound (227 grams) hard fat
2 stalks fresh lemongrass
50 whole fresh lime leaves
7 bulbs fresh shallot
14 cloves fresh garlic
2 stalks fresh green onion (green part only)
3 whole Thai chili peppers
¾ cup (188 milliliters) low-fat milk powder
½ cup (125 milliliters) water
Safflower oil, for frying
Sticky rice, for serving (page 211)
Jeow som, for serving (page 197)

CASING INGREDIENTS

28-millimeter natural pork casing
1½ teaspoons baking soda

SPECIAL EQUIPMENT

Metal mixing bowls
Meat grinder
Stand mixer
Sharp knife
Sausage stuffer
Sheet pans

DAY 1

TRIM MEAT

Trim the brisket of any silver skin and discard. Cube the trimmed meat into 1-inch pieces. Place the cubed meat into a nonreactive food-safe container, such as a wide mixing bowl.

SEASON MEAT

Stir together the table salt, curing salt, and black pepper until well blended.

Pour the salt and pepper blend over the cubed meat, then use your hands to toss the meat with the spices until all pieces are well coated. If any spices fall to the bottom of the container, continue to toss until the spices are adhering.

OVERNIGHT REST

Cover the meat and refrigerate it overnight.

RINSE CASINGS

At the sink, rinse the casings in warm water until any visible salt has been removed. Fill a quart-size container with warm water and the baking soda.

Stir until the soda is combined, then place the rinsed casings in the water. Let them sit in the water overnight.

DAY 2

GRINDING

For this step, you'll be using your grinder. You will also need another mixing bowl or sheet pan to place at the base of the grinder.

Before grinding, toss the meat with any seasonings that may have fallen to the bottom of the container, then place the seasoned meat in the freezer.

Cube the hard fat into 1-inch pieces, and place it in the freezer with the meat.

Also place in the freezer the metal parts of the grinder, which include the grinder plate, the blade, the hopper, the augur, and the cover. Keep everything in the freezer for 30 minutes so they can become cold.

While everything chills, set up your grinder and your station. Place a mixing bowl or sheet pan at the base of the grinder to receive the ground meat.

Gather the fresh lemongrass, lime leaves, fresh shallot, and fresh garlic cloves. Lightly chop, mix, and salt these ingredients and mix together.

After 30 minutes, remove the grinder parts from the freezer and assemble your grinder.

Remove the meat from the freezer and begin grinding. You want to go slowly so the meat doesn't overheat. Working in batches, fill the hopper with several cubes of the meat, a handful of the fresh ingredients, and a couple of the fat cubes, in that order.

Turn on the grinder and let the grinder pull the meat through. If you need to tamp it down, do it gently, and don't force the meat through the grinder. Let the motor (or the crank) do the heavy work.

Continue to feed the meat, fresh ingredients, and fat into the hopper until all of it has been ground.

MIXING THE SAUSAGE PASTE

Place the ground meat in the freezer. If you're using a stand mixer, place the mixer's mixing bowl and flat beater into the freezer with the meat so it can also chill. If you'll be using your hands, place a clean mixing bowl in the freezer. Place the liquid you'll be using in the freezer too.

Allow everything to chill for 30 minutes.

Meanwhile, cut the green part of the green onion into ¼-inch slices. Stem and seed the Thai chilies, and finely dice.

After 30 minutes, remove everything from the freezer. Place the ground meat into the mixing bowl. Add the green onion, Thai chili, milk powder, and chilled liquid. If using a stand mixer, attach the flat beater and beat on medium-low speed until a thick and sticky paste is formed, about 5 minutes.

If using your hands, blend the mixture with your hands until a sticky, well-blended paste is formed, about 10 minutes.

To test whether it's ready, take a small handful of the mixed sausage paste and pat it flat into your palm. Turn your palm over—if the meat adheres to your hand, it's ready for stuffing. If it slips off, however, keep grinding.

TASTE TEST

After mixing and before stuffing, you can do a taste test to see if the seasonings are to your liking.

Heat up a skillet on medium and add a teaspoon of safflower oil. Take a tablespoon-size portion of the mixed sausage paste and form it into a patty. Cook the test patty for 5 to 7 minutes, turning once, or until it's browned and beginning to crisp.

Taste the patty. If you feel it needs any seasoning adjustments, add these to the mixer with the sausage paste and then mix until well blended.

Repeat as desired.

Once you're happy with the sausage paste, place it in the freezer while you set up your casings and stuffing station.

CASING PREP BEFORE STUFFING

Remove the soaked casings from the refrigerator. Dump out the water, then rinse the casings at the sink in warm water.

Fill a clean container with warm water, and place the casings in there until you are ready to use them.

STUFFING

Assemble your stuffer.

If using a vertical dedicated stuffer, remove the sausage paste from the freezer and fill the hopper with the meat. Clamp down the piston so the air bubbles can escape.

If using a stand mixer or grinder with a stuffing attachment, fill the feed tube with the amount it will hold, pressing down to remove any air bubbles.

Take a 3-foot portion of casing (if your casings are longer, you can cut off a portion with a sharp knife). Wet the horn and then slide on all the casing (for more detail, see page 99). Gently pull an inch of the casing off the end of the horn.

Press the meat through the hopper until you see a small bit of meat exit through the horn into the casing. Tie off the end, then proceed with stuffing the casing. (For more details and troubleshooting, see page 98.)

Once the casing is stuffed, repeat for the remainder of the sausage paste.

Form links down the length of the casing (see pages 98–100). After you form the links, with a sharp knife cut off the individual links, then place the sausages on a sheet pan. Allow to rest uncovered overnight in the refrigerator.

Any unused casings can be dried, repacked in salt, covered with water, and refrigerated until you are ready to use them. They should keep for a year, but check what your package recommends.

DAY 3

Set up your smoker for cold smoking (see page 183).

Cold smoke the links and then reheat before serving. Serve with sticky rice and jeow som.

YIELD: 8 POUNDS SAUSAGE

LAO TEXAS SAUSAGE, SHORT VERSION

Cube the meat then combine with the table salt, curing salt, and black pepper until well blended. Refrigerate overnight.

Soak the casings overnight.

The second day, cube the hard fat. Chill the seasoned meat in the freezer for 30 minutes.

Chop the lemongrass, lime leaves, shallot, and garlic, then blend together.

Remove the seasoned meat from the freezer, and grind the meat with a handful of the chopped fresh ingredients and cubed fat. Place the ground meat in the freezer again for 30 minutes.

Cut the green part of the green onion into ¼-inch slices. Stem and seed the Thai chilies, and finely dice.

After chilling, remove the ground meat from the freezer. Mix the ground meat, green onion, Thai chili, milk powder, and liquid until a sticky paste is formed.

Stuff the sausage paste into the casing. Form into links, then cut the individual links. Rest the sausage overnight uncovered in the refrigerator.

The third day, prepare your smoker for cold smoking. Cold smoke the sausages and then reheat before serving (see page 183).

KENNEDALE BEERWURST

We didn't always have beerwurst on our menu. But after Lane came up with a German-style sausage that blended dark stout beer, handfuls of garlic, and warm, sweet spices such as allspice and cinnamon, we knew it deserved a spot on the menu.

Now, what to call this sausage was a big question. At first, Lane called it a bierwurst. The German translation of *bierwurst* is "beer sausage." However, in Germany that sausage doesn't contain any beer. Instead, it's known as such only because it's meant to be served with beer.

No matter! We've never been sticklers for names, so we decided to give a nod to both its Texan and its German roots. Whatever you call it, know that this sausage's warmth, smoke, and gentle heat is like pulling up to the firebox with a folding camp chair.

SAUSAGE INGREDIENTS

2¼ pounds (1.13 kilograms) boneless pork butt
1¾ pounds (794 grams) brisket trim
2 tablespoons table salt
1 teaspoon number one pink curing salt
1½ tablespoons garlic powder
1½ tablespoons onion powder
1 tablespoon white pepper
1 tablespoon mustard powder
1½ tablespoons red pepper flakes
1 teaspoon dried thyme
1 teaspoon ground bay leaf
1½ teaspoons ground nutmeg
1½ teaspoons ground cinnamon
1½ teaspoons ground allspice
1 pound (454 grams) hard brisket fat
25 cloves fresh garlic
½ cup (125 milliliters) water
½ cup (125 milliliters) stout beer
¾ cup (188 milliliters) milk powder
Safflower oil, for frying

CASING INGREDIENTS

28-millimeter natural pork casing
1½ teaspoons baking soda

SPECIAL EQUIPMENT

Metal mixing bowls
Meat grinder
Stand mixer
Sharp knife
Sausage stuffer
Sheet pans

DAY 1

TRIM MEAT

Trim the pork and brisket of any silver skin, and discard. Cube the trimmed meat into 1-inch pieces. Place the cubed meat into a nonreactive food-safe container, such as a wide mixing bowl.

SEASON MEAT

Stir together the table salt, curing salt, garlic powder, onion powder, white pepper, mustard powder, red pepper flakes, dried thyme, ground bay leaf, ground nutmeg, ground cinnamon, and ground allspice until well blended.

Pour the spice blend over the cubed meat, then use your hands to toss the meat with the spices until all pieces are well coated. If any spices fall to the bottom of the container, continue to toss until the spices are adhering.

OVERNIGHT REST

Cover the meat and refrigerate it overnight.

RINSE CASINGS

At the sink, rinse the casings in warm water until any visible salt has been removed. Fill a quart-size container with warm water and the baking soda.

Stir until the soda is combined, then place the rinsed casings in the water. Let them sit in the water overnight.

DAY 2

GRINDING

For this step, you'll be using your grinder. You will also need another mixing bowl or sheet pan to place at the base of the grinder.

Before grinding, toss the meat with any seasonings that may have fallen to the bottom of the container, then place the seasoned meat in the freezer.

Cube the hard fat into 1-inch pieces, and place it in the freezer with the meat.

Also place in the freezer the metal parts of the grinder, which include the grinder plate, the blade, the hopper, the augur, and the cover. Keep everything in the freezer for 30 minutes so they can become cold.

While everything chills, set up your grinder and your station. Place a mixing bowl or sheet pan at the base of the grinder to receive the ground meat.

Gather your garlic cloves.

After 30 minutes, remove the grinder parts from the freezer and assemble your grinder.

Remove the meat from the freezer and begin grinding. You want to go slowly so the meat doesn't overheat. Working in batches, fill the hopper with several cubes of the meat, a couple of the garlic cloves, and a couple of the fat cubes, in that order.

Turn on the grinder and let the grinder pull the meat through. If you need to tamp it down, do it gently, and don't force the meat through the grinder. Let the motor (or the crank) do the heavy work.

Continue to feed the meat, garlic, and fat into the hopper until all of it has been ground.

MIXING THE SAUSAGE PASTE

Place the ground meat in the freezer. If you're using

a stand mixer, place the mixer's mixing bowl and flat beater in the freezer with the meat so it can also chill. If you'll be using your hands, place a clean mixing bowl in the freezer. Place the water and stout you'll be using in the freezer too.

Allow everything to chill for 30 minutes.

After 30 minutes, remove everything from the freezer. Place the ground meat into the mixing bowl. Add the milk powder and the chilled water and stout. If using a stand mixer, attach the flat beater and beat on medium-low speed until a thick and sticky paste is formed, about 5 minutes.

If using your hands, blend the mixture with your hands until a sticky, well-blended paste is formed, about 10 minutes.

To test whether it's ready, take a small handful of the mixed sausage paste and pat it flat into your palm. Turn your palm over—if the meat adheres to your hand, it's ready for stuffing. If it slips off, however, keep grinding.

TASTE TEST

After mixing and before stuffing, you can do a taste test to see if the seasonings are to your liking.

Heat up a skillet on medium and add a teaspoon of safflower oil. Take a tablespoon-size portion of the mixed sausage paste and form it into a patty. Cook the test patty for 5 to 7 minutes, turning once, or until it's browned and beginning to crisp.

Taste the patty. If you feel the sausage needs any seasoning adjustments, add these to the mixer with the sausage paste and then mix until well blended.

Repeat as desired.

Once you're happy with the sausage paste, place it in the freezer while you set up your casings and stuffing station.

CASING PREP BEFORE STUFFING

Remove the soaked casings from the refrigerator. Dump out the water, then rinse the casings at the sink in warm water.

Fill a clean container with warm water, and place the casings in there until you are ready to use them.

STUFFING

Assemble your stuffer.

If using a vertical dedicated stuffer, remove the sausage paste from the freezer and fill the hopper with the meat. Clamp down the piston so the air bubbles can escape.

If using a stand mixer or grinder with a stuffing attachment, fill the feed tube with the amount it will hold, pressing down to remove any air bubbles.

Take a 3-foot portion of casing (if your casings are longer, you can cut off a portion with a sharp knife). Wet the horn and then slide on all of the casing (for more detail, see page 99). Gently pull an inch of the casing off the end of the horn.

Press the meat through the hopper until you see a small bit of meat exit through the horn into the casing. Tie off the end, then proceed with stuffing the casing. (For more details and troubleshooting, see page 98.)

Once the casing is stuffed, repeat for the remainder of the sausage paste.

Form links down the length of the casing (see pages 98–100). After you form the links, with a sharp knife cut off the individual links, then place the sausages on a sheet pan. Allow to rest uncovered overnight in the refrigerator.

Any unused casings can be dried, repacked in salt, covered with water, and refrigerated until you are ready to use them. They should keep for a year, but check what your package recommends.

DAY 3

Set up your smoker for cold smoking (see page 183).

Cold smoke the links and then reheat before serving.

YIELD: 5 POUNDS SAUSAGE

KENNEDALE BEERWURST, SHORT VERSION

Cube the meat, then combine with the table salt, curing salt, garlic powder, onion powder, white pepper, mustard powder, red pepper flakes, dried thyme, ground bay leaf, ground nutmeg, ground cinnamon, and ground allspice until well blended. Refrigerate overnight.

Soak the casings overnight.

The second day, cube the hard fat. Chill the seasoned meat in the freezer for 30 minutes.

Remove the seasoned meat from the freezer, and grind the meat with the garlic cloves and cubed fat. Place the ground meat in the freezer again for 30 minutes with the water and stout.

After chilling, remove the ground meat from the freezer. Mix the ground meat, milk powder, water, and stout until a sticky paste is formed.

Stuff the sausage paste into the casing. Form into links, then cut the individual links. Rest the sausage overnight uncovered in the refrigerator.

The third day, prepare your smoker for cold smoking. Cold smoke the sausages and then reheat before serving (see page 183).

Goldee's
BAR-B-Q

PITMASTER PROFILE

JALEN HEARD

If you look up *Jalen* in the dictionary of names, you'll see that it means tranquil and calm, or in the parlance of today's kids—chill. No one has ever had a more appropriate name than Jalen Heard, as he is indeed the calm center of the Goldee's team.

For instance, if you need a small task taken care of immediately, he'll grab the toolbox. If you need someone to work a double bread shift and shape hundreds of loaves of bread in one night, he'll assemble his station with dough, a scale, and pans. If you need someone to explain the minutia of preparing sausage, he'll come up with an interactive discussion that will leave his students instant experts. More importantly, he'll most likely do all of these things with good humor and a smile.

As sincere as Jalen can be, he's been known to play pranks. When he began dating a new woman, he hatched a plan that he would tell everyone that he was so in love, he was going to propose. One apprentice, in all of her older-woman wisdom, cautioned him to go slow, but he kept insisting he was ready to buy a ring and elope.

It turned out that the guys found humor in this, and the apprentice laughed too. A few months later, when Jalen brought the same woman to a Goldee's party, the apprentice could see that he was indeed clearly in love with this woman, and while he may have been joking, there was something there.

This sweet, playful energy has made Jalen a favorite of many. When he walks into the kitchen, everyone looks up and says, "Jalen!" When he goes out in Fort Worth or Dallas, people will recognize him and either shout his name, if they know it, or wave and say, "Goldee's!" He is the man about town.

Restaurant cooks have a habit of saying, "Heard!" when a request is delivered in the kitchen. This lets the person giving the order know that their words were received. At Goldee's, however, when the chorus of "heards" begins, inevitably someone will shout, "Jalen!"—which always breaks any tension and reestablishes a chill tone.

"Heard," of course, is also Jalen's last name, hence someone saying "Jalen" upon hearing it at Goldee's. While it's a joke, there's also some truth in it. Asking people to do things can be difficult, and finding that balance between leadership and pettiness can be tricky. But if you add a "Jalen" to your "heard," then the goal will be achieved much more harmoniously.

Imagine if restaurant cooks everywhere said, "Jalen!" after they said, "Heard!" Imagine how chill and calm every restaurant kitchen could be. That is the power of Jalen Heard.

7 ON THE SMOKER

MILL SCALE
METAL WORKS
LOCKHART, TX
300
250
200
150
100
50

Our meat rep stopped by while the team was trimming briskets. At the table were Jalen, Lane, and Jonny.

"Are you running an apprentice shop here?" said the meat rep to the table. Jonny admitted that they were, adding that their aim was to open up satellites around the world, bringing good barbecue to all.

While the person pulling the meat off the smoker sometimes gets the most attention, the true pitmaster work begins in the kitchen with your knife. We start everyone in the same place. If you can perfectly trim a brisket, then your work is almost done.

Cooking on the smoker is at the heart of what we do, and while we are equally thrilled with our side dishes, pickles, bread, and desserts, without smoked meats we would not be a barbecue restaurant. Cooking on smokers defines who we are.

It's not a challenge to smoke meat, though if you want it to be juicy and tender with a solid, crunchy bark, there are steps you'll need to take. Each of our recipes presented here will walk you through every step of the cook. These are the guidelines we follow, and they will work equally well if you're cooking on a 1,000-gallon professional smoker or a 94-gallon backyard rig.

Sure, some elements will change due to the number of meats being smoked or the size of the firebox, chamber, and smokestack. But once you get into the flow and learn what makes your smoker cook the way you want it to, then our methods will work just as well for you at home as they do for us at Goldee's.

Don't skip any of the steps, because each is designed to build on the previous one. Now, some methods, such as smoking turkey, have fewer steps than smoking a brisket. But none of the methods are challenging; they only need to be done with intention and with a goal in mind.

Anyone can cook barbecue. All you need is a smoker and the desire to give it a go. At Goldee's, we believe that anyone can smoke meats, and we'll gladly hand the shovel to anyone willing to give it a try.

BRISKET

As we were pulling and wrapping briskets after the all-day cook, one apprentice asked the pitmaster if she could identify who had trimmed each. She laughed, pointed at a brisket with a sharp, flat edge on the lean rounding out to a graceful curve, and said, "Lane did this one." She was correct.

Trimming the brisket is the first step in the brisket-cook process. As the meat cooks, it loses almost 30 percent of its weight as the fat renders and the excess liquid evaporates out of the meat.

Yet as it shrinks, it still retains its former shape. Each brisket has its own signature, given to it by the hands that worked with it throughout the cook.

This is our secret at Goldee's. While many places treat their briskets like nameless, faceless slabs of beef, we coax the essence out of each by giving it heaps of attention from the beginning to the end.

First, we use natural briskets that are hormone-free, from cows that have lived a decent life. That immediately sets your meat way above commodity-grade beef that has been treated with no love or respect.

Next, we don't use prime grade but instead go with choice. It's a higher grade of choice than regular choice, but our point is that it's not the fancy grade of meat that determines your success, but what you do with the beef. We treat our choice briskets as if they were the finest grade of meat, and it shows when the job is done. They have been given much love and respect.

When we trim our briskets, we give them an aerodynamic shape so they can go with the flow. There are no sharp angles or jagged edges to disrupt the constant motion of smoke and heat as it moves through the cooking chamber. Instead, the movement of air is continuous, which helps the brisket cook evenly.

We want to champion the rich, beefy flavor of brisket, so we season it simply. There is just enough salt, just enough pepper, and just enough seasonings for the brisket to turn out just right. When applying the seasonings, we also think about the brisket's future size and shape after its time in the smoker. This helps us to not go under or over in our seasoning. Again, it comes out just right.

We build gentle fires that are hot enough but not too hot. And when it's time to push the brisket out of its complacency and move it from the stall (we'll explain what the stall is later) into the final stage, we dial up the heat just enough to render that top fat and get it done.

There's a reason why our brisket is our ideal brisket, and if you follow our steps, you will understand the process. From there, you can take each brisket and make it your own. And how beautiful will that be, to have your own incredible brisket in the world?

STEP 1: TOOLS

Large cutting board
6-inch boning knife
Spray bottle filled with warm water
Instant-read thermometer
1-cup measuring cup
Foil
10-inch serrated knife

You will need a large cutting board to trim the brisket. Since we're not removing any bones, we use a sharp boning knife to remove the fat and shape the meat. We use the thermometer to tell the internal temperature of the brisket, though we use the probe to feel the brisket's tenderness, too, which is also a guide. The measuring cup will be used at the end of the cook to pour melted tallow onto foil, which will then be wrapped around the cooked brisket before it rests. The tallow adds moisture and shine to the final product.

STEP 2: MEAT

1 packer-cut choice brisket, 10–15 pounds

Now, we know that a lot of you have probably heard that prime-grade meat is really, really good, but it's harder to make a good brisket from it because there's so much internal fat. It not only takes more time to render all that fat properly but it also comes out tasting less beefy. Don't even get us started on Wagyu!

This is why we prefer choice. It's a lot easier for us to render all the internal fat, which is one of your main goals. And the flavor is more rich and savory. Your brisket, if you use choice, will taste like beef.

We get our all-natural choice briskets from Creekstone, but we've also cooked plenty of grocery store briskets, and you can get the same results if you take care when choosing your brisket.

When you're shopping at the store, you want to buy what's called a packer cut. This will be in the meat section, and it will be a 10-to-15-pound slab of meat wrapped in plastic. If you don't see them out on display, ask the butcher if they have any in the back. You can also find them at big-box stores such as Walmart and Costco.

Take some time to go through the available briskets, since they're not all the same. First, you want to get one that has a full coverage of fat on the fatty side with no *scalps*, which is our term for meat showing through the fat cap because it's been aggressively trimmed. Because of this, we also recommend avoiding a pretrimmed brisket since you'll want to trim it to our specs and not the store's.

For the lean, assess the *marbling*, which is the term for the blend of red meat and white fat. You want to see some lines of fat going through the meat. But even if it doesn't have too much, you can still work with it. The fat cap, however, is the most important consideration. If there's a nice layer of fat on top, we know that we'll be turning out a pretty good brisket, regardless of the marbling.

Also, try to find one with a similar thickness on both sides, and look for a brisket with a balanced amount of point muscle and lean. These qualities in the meat will help you cook the brisket more evenly.

STEP 3: TRIMMING

First, moisten a hand towel and place it on a flat surface, such as your kitchen counter or a table. The towel will keep the cutting board from moving as you trim. Next, place a large cutting board on top. As we said in chapter 3, at the restaurant we use plastic cutting boards, but whatever you have that is large enough for the brisket will work.

Sharpen your boning knife, which is the tool we recommend for trimming a brisket, and keep your sharpener close to your trimming station since you may want to touch up the blade's edge as you trim. The sharper the knife, the easier it is to make cuts. Also, a dull knife is more prone to slip and cause accidents. (We have a first-aid kit stocked with bandages just in case the knife slips and gets one of our fingers instead of the fat.)

Have extra hand towels or paper towels on hand to mop up the blood, and wipe your blade as you cut. Place a trash can close to your station, and to save the fat and trim for tallow (page 201), sausage (page 183), and chili (page 216), we recommend having separate receptacles for each. For instance, as we trim, we throw the fat for tallow into a pot, the meat for sausage into one bin, and any lean for chili into another bin.

Now that you have your station prepared, take your brisket from the refrigerator. (You want your brisket to be cold when you're trimming, as this makes the work much easier.) Most likely, your brisket will be wrapped in plastic, as this is how packer briskets are sold.

If you can see through the plastic, you'll notice that one side is covered in a layer of fat and the other side has only patches of fat mixed with the meat. You want to slice open the package with your sharp knife on the side with less fat. This is the bottom of the brisket, so if you accidentally cut into it as you open the package, it won't affect the final bark formation on the top.

After you cut into the package, you'll probably be deluged with red liquid. While it may appear to be blood, it's actually myoglobin, which is the protein that gives meat its color. It's messy, but don't worry. Just grab one of your towels and soak it up from the board and surface. Lift the brisket out of the plastic and place it fat-side down on the cutting board, then throw the plastic away and wipe up any more liquid. You are now ready to trim.

There are many ways to approach the brisket, but we begin on the back side. Before we get into that, however, let's talk about this slab of beef. You'll notice that there is a thicker portion of the brisket and a thinner part.

If you squint and look at the brisket from the side, you could say that it's somewhat shaped like a hatchback car. The back, bulky end is called the point or fatty end, and the thinner end is called the flat or the lean. It's also illustrative to say that it looks like a 3D map, with the point being the mountainous area that slopes down into the flatter lands of the lean.

On the fatty end, you'll see on one side another ridge that runs up from about the center of the brisket to the tip. We call this piece the mohawk, as it's shaped like that hairstyle that has a raised ridge running down the center of one's skull. (After we were named number one by *Texas Monthly*, Jonny got an adapted mohawk haircut. He said it was to celebrate his beloved Atlanta Braves winning the World Series that year, though we also suspected it was in honor of one of his favorite things to cook.)

Looking at the point, the side adjacent to the mohawk side is what we call the money bites. We'll talk about this more later, but this patch of beef, once cooked, holds the most delectable and primo cuts.

The far edge will form the burnt ends, which if you've visited Goldee's, you've been offered when waiting in line. It's a juicy, crispy (the good kind of crispy), meltingly tender piece of brisket. People often swoon when taking a bite. And then they order more brisket, hence the name "money bites." The other slices you will get from this side are also excellent. Keep this in mind when trimming and cooking. This is your most precious real estate on the brisket.

If you look at the brisket like it's a 3D map, then the center of the brisket is about where the point begins to slope down into the flat. We'll come back to this.

Okay, let's begin to trim. First, start on the back side of the brisket. If you look on the point end, you'll see a large area of fat underneath the money bites side that is about the size of a hand. This is the deckle.

Place your finger on it, and you'll feel that it's hard. This is not edible as is, so we remove it. To do this, hold your knife parallel with the brisket, then run the knife under this bit of fat and slice it off the back. You may need to do this in a couple of passes. If you're saving your fat to make sausage, you can throw this hard fat in the proper receptacle, as it's the best fat for blending with meat for sausage.

Assess the rest of the back side to see if there are any dangling pieces of fat. If so, remove those too. We don't worry too much about the silver skin, though, since it's just going to render out as the meat cooks.

Now, flip the brisket over to the fatty side. This is where most of the work will happen.

The next cut is removing the mohawk. The key is to get the point end of the brisket as close to the same level as the lean so it will cook evenly.

If you run your hand over the mohawk starting at the tip, you'll feel that this hump ends in about the center of the brisket. Beginning at the center, use your knife to start cutting off the mohawk, running the knife parallel to the brisket from the center to the tip. Your aim is to level out the point end, so that's the depth you'll want to cut. This piece can be used for sausage.

Once the mohawk is gone, turn the brisket one turn so that the point is facing up and the lean is closest to you. We are going to trim the sides to make the shape of the brisket more even.

Starting close to the center where the mohawk ended, on the side, slice downward a half inch running down from the center to the tip of the lean. You can save this meat for sausage or chili. Repeat this cut on the other side of the brisket, the money bites side, again starting where the point ends in the center.

Along the bottom of the brisket, you'll want to round off the shape. An easy way to do this is to draw with your knife the U-shape that will create this final form, then make the incision. This meat can be used for sausage or chili.

Okay, now it's time to remove some fat. Starting on the money bites side of the point, you'll probably see a lot of fat. One tip we offer to beginners is to cut a slit into this fat, wedge it open with your finger, and look down. This way, you can get an idea of how much fat you'll need to trim. We like to keep about a ¼-inch layer of fat on top of the meat, so if you see an inch, for instance, you'll want to trim ¾ inch off to reach that point.

To trim the fat, run your knife down each area you're working on (it's easier to work in small sections instead of trying to do the entire length of the brisket in one fell swoop), and just lightly shave the fat off with your knife. Keep making gentle strokes until you take off as much fat as you want. This fat can be used for tallow.

Once you're happy with the amount of fat removed (you can keep doing the incision test to see how much) from the point, now it's time to move down to the flat. Since you've trimmed the sides off the brisket, you've most likely opened it up to where you can see the layer of fat on the side of the lean. This will give you a guide for trimming from this section. However, the fat on the lean may not run evenly, so don't cut too aggressively or you may scalp the brisket.

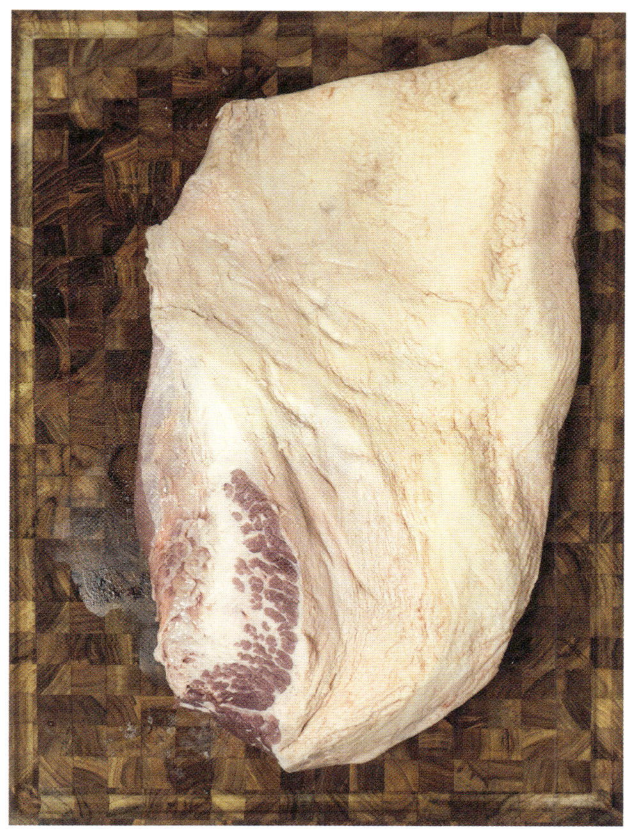

An untrimmed brisket fatty side.

An untrimmed brisket, back side.

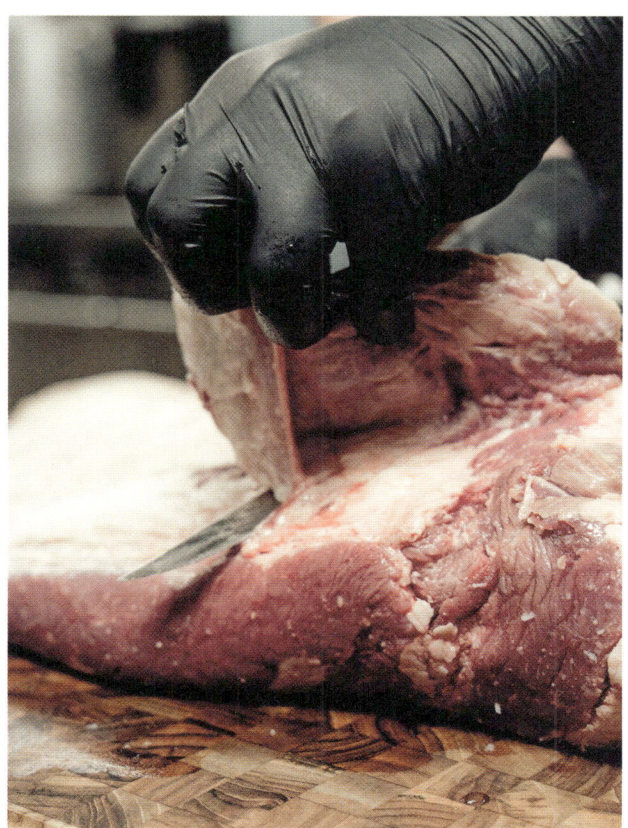

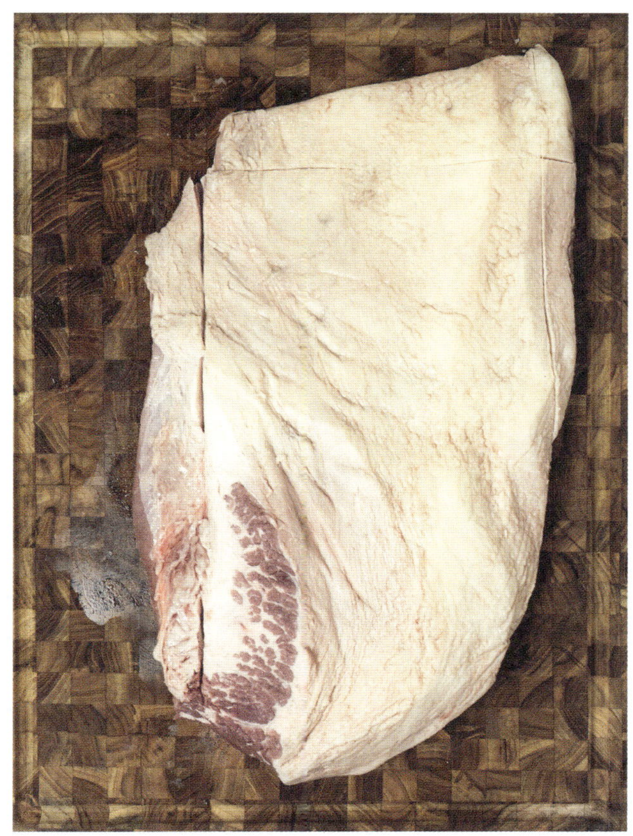

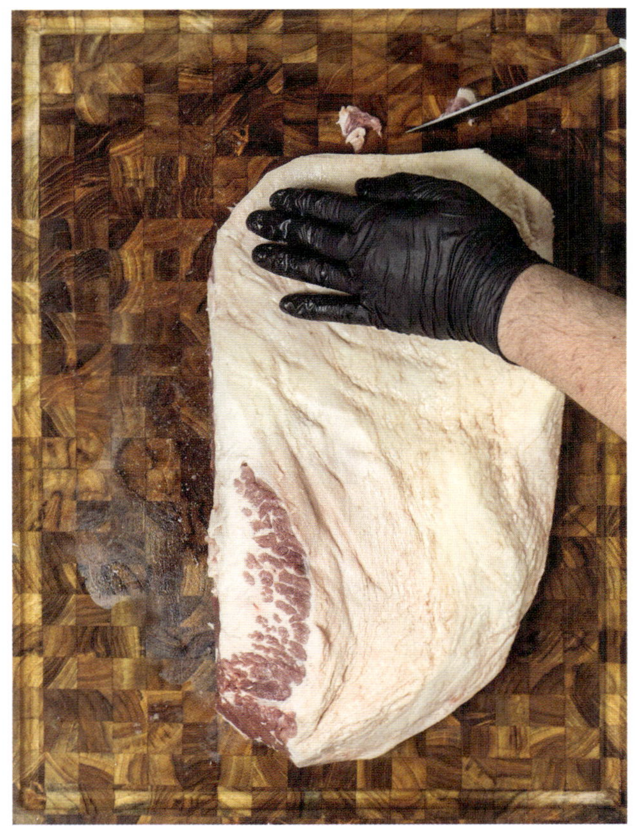
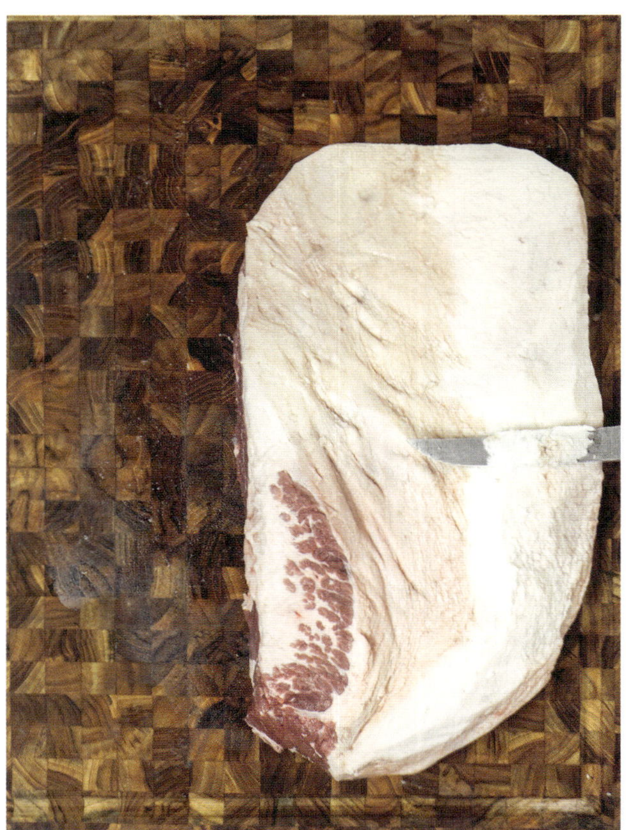

Scalping is the term we use for when you've taken off too much fat and you can now see the meat. Don't fret if this happens, as even we do it sometimes! Just keep cutting and try to avoid doing it again.

When you're satisfied with the fat cover on the lean, you now need to go into the center of the brisket and do some more excavation.

The way this cut of meat is formed is that the lean runs almost the length of the brisket. The point is layered on top of the lean, which means that on some cuts you'll have fatty brisket on top and lean on the bottom. In between will be a line of fat.

Where the point begins to rise on top of the lean is close to the center. It's here that there may be additional patches of fat on the cap, and you'll want to go in and scoop those out so you can get close to your ¼ inch layer of fat. As for the line of fat that runs internally between the two muscles, the goal is to render that out as you cook.

When we're pleased with the amount of fat removed, we like to finesse the shape some more. Look at the tip of the point. You want it to be round, so if it's an odd shape, round it out. Do the same with the bottom of the lean—see if it needs any more trims to get the shape that you want. Ultimately, if you're looking at your brisket from above, it should be shaped like a bean.

STEP 4: SEASONING

Squeeze bottle with water
Coarse black pepper
Table salt
Seasoned salt (page 200)

The rumors are true, and we did indeed use Lawry's seasoned salt on pretty much everything we cooked when we first opened. After we were named number one, though, we were contacted by a copacker about making our own seasoned salt to sell. We took that opportunity to develop our own seasoned salt blend, which you can make at home or buy from us online or at the restaurant. If you use it, your brisket will have the same flavor as ours, though we still recommend Lawry's, too, if that's what you prefer.

Even though we offer a blend of pepper with salt, we still take the time to season with each separately. We start with coarse-ground black pepper, then we add a layer of table salt, and we finish with the seasoned salt. We go in that order because the salt granules are smaller than the pepper, and if you started with those, the pepper would not stick.

We prefer table salt because it's easier for us to maintain control. Kosher salt has larger flakes, and when you're seasoning fifty briskets at a time, it's hard to be precise. We want every slice to be well seasoned, and we've found that table salt makes it easier to get an even coating in a shorter amount of time. It also sticks better to the meat and ensures that each bite will have a blast of salt, which carries all the other flavors. You want to use a lighter hand with table salt than you would with kosher salt, but its advantages outweigh this one quirk.

To recap, the sequence is pepper, table salt, and then seasoned salt. You can get creative with that last layer of flavor that you put on. For instance, if you wanted, you could use garlic salt or celery salt or some other kind of mixture to cut through the base of pepper and salt. You can do a lot of cool stuff to make your brisket super unique to you.

To start, we spritz the brisket with water. In our early days, we used our standard binder of mustard and pickle juice, but now we only use mustard and water.

You need only a little liquid to help the seasonings adhere, and for the long brisket cook, we found that what we used didn't make a difference in terms of flavor.

If you prefer, you can use the mustard and water binder we recommend for beef ribs (page 150), but the water does the same thing. It's also easier to spread, so you're less likely to have clumps, which we found with the mustard. Water is a lot easier to use, and it's free! You could use pretty much anything as a binder for the brisket, but because you won't taste it at the end, it's not all that important. Our briskets' flavor comes from our seasoning and the smoke.

For our seasoning, we begin on the bottom of the brisket. You want to do this side first because you want to have a clean slate on top. Your key focus will be on the brisket's top because that's where the flavor will develop. Most of the bottom seasonings will melt away during the cook, so we don't waste our seasoned salt there. We don't get too wild when seasoning the bottom side.

Our first pass will be with the pepper. We hold the shaker at eye level and then, starting at one end, sprinkle the pepper evenly across the brisket until we reach the other end. You don't want to go too heavy with the pepper because as the brisket cooks, it will shrink. You want to see some space between the seasoning; don't blanket the brisket in black.

The second pass on the bottom will be with the table salt. Using the same technique, do one pass across the entire bottom of the brisket. Gently pat the bottom of the brisket all over to set the pepper and salt.

Flip the brisket over. Spritz the top with the water, and again start with the pepper. Do one pass with the pepper, again nothing too crazy. You want to see some of the fat in between the black grains, and you want it also to be even. Again, as the brisket cooks, it shrinks, and the pepper creates a shell. If there's too much, the pepper will begin to flake off the meat. So, it's very important to leave some space in between the pepper so it stays on the meat.

The pepper also helps with the bark formation. It attracts a lot of smoke and helps the smoke flavor stick to the brisket. If you didn't use pepper, it would come out brown, but the pepper is what gives the brisket its distinctive black bark.

This smoke attraction is why we don't season the sides of the brisket. We know that sounds kind of weird, but we feel like the smoke will dry out the sides because they're not covered in fat. So, we don't season the sides.

Of course, if you get a little bit of seasoning on the sides, it's fine. We used to season the sides. After we tried it without seasoning, however, we realized that the edges came out more juicy because they weren't attracting as much smoke and heat, which causes the meat to dry. You do want that smoky heat on the top because it gives you a nice bark and will render the fat really nicely.

Next, we add the table salt with one nice, light pass. We eyeball everything, so it's hard to give you exact measurements, but this first pass of the table salt is going to be your base.

Now, some would say that after this first pass, the brisket is nicely seasoned. But we wrap our briskets with tallow for extra moisture, and the additional oils mute the salt, so an extra pass ensures it won't be too bland. This last pass of salt cuts through the tallow bath and gives each cut the perfect amount of saltiness.

The seasoned salt isn't as salty as the table salt alone, so you can now layer a pretty good amount on the brisket. You're looking for a nice orangey color, and then you're going to pat it all in to make sure it sticks into that fat really well.

On the point, we are more aggressive with the fatty side versus the Mohawk side, because the fatty side is the prime cut of the brisket. When you're done, you're just looking for a nice orange coat. Gently pat it all in and now you have a nicely seasoned brisket!

Of course, there are a lot of ways to be creative with this and make it your own. What you do with that final layer is really up to you. Only you know what's going to make it taste how you'd like it.

Now, if you choose to use preblended salt and pepper, the key is to keep shaking the container to keep everything even. The pepper tends to sink, and not only will it end up on top but the blend also won't be evenly divided between the salt and pepper.

This is why we moved to seasoning the brisket with each ingredient separately—so we could fine-tune exactly how much of each seasoning was going onto the briskets. This keeps the ratio perfect and consistent.

Of course, you may be saying, "Don't you sell pre-mixed blends?" Yes, we do! But we also believe ours are loosely packed, and if you're doing only one brisket, the constant shaking to keep everything evenly distributed won't be a hassle. We found, however, that it took too much time with fifty briskets because we were constantly shaking.

STEP 5: PLACEMENT ON THE SMOKER

Our goal when loading the briskets on our offset smoker is to stay as far from the fire as we can. The closer you get to the fire, the more direct the heat. You can do the long cook that a brisket requires in an offset because it's more gentle. We want to keep the meat away from the fire and have a gentle flow of air.

As the briskets shrink throughout the cook, we keep shifting them away from the fire because we don't want them to burn. They shrink pretty quickly, so we typically do about two shifts per cook.

We don't rotate our meats; we only move them away from the fire and closer to the smokestack as they cook. Having our firebox door almost closed and the damper partway closed helps trap the heat, which then circulates and fills the entire smoker. This keeps the temperature even all over, and we find that the cook is more consistent this way.

A fully open damper would pull the heat and smoke so fast that they wouldn't have time to fill the entire chamber and reach each meat evenly. That said, no smoker is perfect—they all will have hot spots.

Once you figure out where the hot spots are by doing a biscuit test (see page 69), you can take extra care when placing your meats. For the most part, we find that the damper and door staying in our preferred positions ensures the most even cook.

When we position our briskets in the smoker, because we're cooking twenty-four on each, we need to grade them by size so we can place them in the most efficient spots. The largest ones will go in the back row, the front row, and along the back wall, as these three places in the smoker tend to be hotter.

The smaller briskets go by the door and in the middle because it doesn't cook as hot there. Also, if the smaller ones are done before the larger ones, having them closer to the door makes it easier to reach them and pull them out of the smoker.

On a backyard smoker, if you don't have a lot of room, the key is to keep the meat as close to the smokestack as possible. This is a good rule no matter the smoker's size! Even if we were cooking only one brisket on the 1,000-gallon, it would still be in the back, closest to the smokestack.

On the backyard smoker, we would keep it in the

middle of the rack, instead of by the door or wall, so it cooks more evenly. However, if you find that it's taking a long time to cook, we recommend moving it closer to the wall, as it will be hotter there.

Throughout the cook, we leave the firebox door open only an inch or so (except when we add logs, when, of course, we open it all the way). This allows enough air to enter to keep the fire going, but it also lets the fire burn longer.

On top of the smokestack, the damper pulls the smoke and heat through the cooking chamber. For our cooks, we prefer to leave it halfway open. For our 1,000-gallon offsets, this works well.

On a smaller backyard smoker, such as ours, you can tinker more to get the effect that you want. The rule of thumb is that the more open the damper, the faster the smoke and heat will travel through the chamber. Your fires will burn faster, which means you'll need more logs. Your cooks will also take longer because the heat won't stay in the smoker.

A fully open damper makes the heat and smoke rip through the smoker. We like to have a slower flow, which helps the meat cook more quickly but also leaves more smoke flavor. Halfway open is a good balance.

Another reason why we leave the firebox and damper in the same position is that helps with troubleshooting your cooks. There are so many variables that if you're constantly changing everything, it will be a challenge to determine where to improve your cook.

For instance, if you do one cook with the damper a quarter of the way open and another cook with it halfway open, those changes plus the opening of the firebox door will make it hard to determine what is causing problems. Keeping the damper and firebox in the same position in every cook makes it easier to dial in your technique since you have fewer variables to adjust.

If your firebox door has a vent, we recommend keeping it closed. The air being pulled through the vent will combust the fire too quickly, and the fire will burn taller and hotter, not lower and slower. Then the flames will get into the smoke chamber and burn your meat. But again, keep the door slightly ajar because if it's closed all the way, the fire won't receive any oxygen and will die. It will also get way too smoky. It's all about balance!

We keep the grease trap open (our smokers don't have a way to close it, but even if they did, we'd leave it open). This is because we want the grease to exit the smoker. It's scary to think of all that fat sliding toward the fire!

STEP 6: FIRE AND SMOKE

We recommend starting your fire when you're prepping your cook. This way, you can start building your coal bed sooner, which will make for an easier, more efficient cook. For the first fire, you can build a log-cabin-style fire or a bundle fire (for more detail, see chapter 5). It's your choice.

Each smoker is different, but for a 90-gallon offset, we'd start with two full logs (or four splits) for the initial burn.

For your first fire, your goal is to start building the coal bed and produce smoke. The coal bed provides a solid foundation for fueling up the new logs you add to the firebox as you cook, and the smoke adds flavor to the meat.

We place the brisket on the smoker while it's still cold, right after seasoning. We'll go into more detail about temperatures in the next section, but we want the smoker to get up to temperature slowly. This helps the brisket to cook more evenly and not tighten up and get crispy.

For your first fire, open the damper all the way. Once the fire is lit, close the firebox door almost all the way, leaving it cracked open about an inch. This will pull the smoke through the chamber and allow the wood to burn down and form your bed of coals.

After an hour or so, ideally your smoker will be up to about 200°F. If it's not, don't worry about it too much—it will get there! At this time, the logs will be burnt. With your shovel, break the burnt logs down. Now you have a coal bed.

Build your next fire in a log cabin style, and we recommend continuing this style for the remainder of the cook. After the initial fire, we also close the damper halfway. This locks in the heat and helps the fat to render more quickly. For the next 10 to 12 hours, you'll be simply breaking down and rebuilding your fires, every half hour or so.

Be sure to clean out the ashes from the firebox if there's too much accumulation along the way because you don't want the logs to rise too high.

We don't use water pans in our large offsets, but with a backyard smoker, if you're worried about burnt edges, you can use a water pan in the first stage of the cook. After this point, we would remove it. There's so much liquid being cooked out of the meat that the chamber, no matter the size, will be humid, and you won't need the extra moisture from the water. You want a drier heat at this point to get through the stall and render all the fat. The fat will render better in the hotter, arid environment.

For those unfamiliar with the term *stall,* it describes a period when the brisket's temperature begins rising at a slower pace than before. This period can last for several hours, and it can be confusing because it appears something has gone wrong with the cook. Nothing has gone wrong! What's happening is that the brisket is releasing tons of liquid, which is what you want (there may be pools of liquid on the flat portion of the brisket, for instance). However, the liquid also is cooling the meat at the same time, so the temperature rises more slowly.

Just as we don't use a water pan, we don't spritz our briskets either. If you want to spritz the brisket in the first two stages instead of using a water pan, you can, but we don't. Once the meat hits the stall, you don't want to spritz anymore because the goal is a nice, crispy bark and the spritz will just add too much moisture.

STEP 7: TIME AND TEMPERATURE

There are four stages in cooking a brisket, with the first three stages lasting about 3 to 4 hours each and the last one about 1 to 2 hours (about 12 hours total). Sometimes it will go faster and sometimes it will be longer, but that's a good guide to follow.

Here's the short version, but we'll also go into more detail about each stage. (Please note that these temperatures may vary if you're not using an offset smoker.)

BRISKET TEMP GUIDE

STAGE 1:
Brisket 40°F to 120°F / Smoker 200°F to 225°F

STAGE 2:
Brisket 120°F to 150°F / Smoker 225°F to 250°F

STAGE 3 (THE STALL):
Brisket 150°F to 170°F / Smoker 250°F to 275°F

STAGE 4 (FINAL PUSH):
Brisket 170°F to 200°F / Smoker 275°F to 300°F

Now, as you cook, you'll want to probe the meat for its internal temperature, but it's also important to take note of the visual cues. Eventually, you'll be able to look at a brisket and know just where it is in the cook.

To train our pitmasters, we once removed the thermometers from our 1,000-gallons so they could learn to cook by instinct. Not one customer complained, so it must have worked! (Jalen calls this cooking Tootsie style in honor of Tootsie Tomanetz, the octogenarian pitmaster at Snow's in Lexington, Texas, who is known for not using thermometers.)

When you're getting started, however, we recommend taking temps. To take temps of the meat, we always probe in the same spot: dead center of the brisket, where the lean meets the point.

We do this because the internal temperature varies across the brisket, with the thin edges on the lean, for instance, being hotter since they cook faster. If you probe only in the center, which is also the coolest spot on the brisket, you will have a consistent benchmark for the entire meat.

For example, if you temped the outer edges, they might read 210°F, but the center would be only 185. If you pulled it based on that outer probe, your brisket wouldn't be done. Because the center is going to have the lowest temperature, we prefer to make all our decisions based on this temperature, as we've found that it's a more accurate gauge for the entire brisket.

Okay, now onto the four stages.

STAGE 1

200–225°F
3–4 hours

The goal of this first stage is to build your coal bed, have the brisket slowly come up to temperature, attract smoke, and begin building your bark. Your target temperature during this time is 200 to 225°F. Don't worry if it's too smoky because that's flavor! Obviously, you don't want to have a super smoky cook the entire 12 hours, but it's fine in Stage 1.

You're also trying to warm up the meat slowly because it's a huge piece of muscle and fat. The outer edges of it will get way hotter than the middle of it if you put it on and go straight to 275°F. It will instantly start cooking unevenly. But if you stay low and you let the big chunk of meat warm up slowly, the entire piece will warm up at the same pace, and then it will continue to cook evenly throughout the entire cook.

It's also important to warm up slowly because it helps the lean. As the lean cooks, it begins to release liquid and curve upward. If you start slower and smokier, then you won't lose your bark on the lean. It will help the bark to stay.

The drier, smokier airflow going through the smoker in this phase will not only give the brisket flavor but also help that fat dry out so the bark can form and stick for the rest of the cook.

If you go straight to 275°F, however, the bark doesn't have time to set. When pools start to form on top of the lean, leave them on the brisket since they will evaporate eventually. We don't recommend draining the liquid off the brisket because it may take the pepper and spices with it, leaving the meat without its bark.

At the end of the first 3 to 4 hours, when you touch the brisket on top, it should be starting to firm up a bit more. It won't feel raw anymore.

STAGE 2

225–250°F

3–4 hours

This next stage is all about getting your brisket to the stall, which we'll go into more detail about in the next section. At this point in the cook, however, you're just seeing the bark continue to form and the brisket shrink. Bump the firebox temperature up 25 degrees, and just keep it even.

You'll know you're through this stage when your brisket is at an internal temperature of 150 to 160°F, which is when the stall begins. You'll also know it's hitting the stall when you see pools of liquid develop on the lean.

While you may be tempted to tilt your brisket to dump off the liquid, don't do this! With that liquid will also go your beautiful bark, so just be patient. As the brisket cooks, that liquid will evaporate.

STAGE 3

250–275°F

3–4 hours

Now it's time to go hotter. If you've been probing your brisket throughout the cook and watching the internal temperature of the meat slowly rise, the stall is when it will stay around 150 to 160°F for what seems like forever—hence the name "the stall."

While we don't know the exact science behind this, what we do know is that the meat stalls while its temperature is rising because as it releases liquid, the liquid is cooling off the meat at the same time.

Think about when you're outside on a hot day and you begin to sweat. Your body releases liquid in its attempt to keep you cool. The brisket is doing the same when it releases liquid.

In this third stage, our goal is to push the brisket harder so it will release as much liquid as it needs to render the fat. You still want to cook it nice and slow and not go *too* hot. But once it's in the stall, you can add more logs to get the temperature up to between 250 and 275°F.

You don't want to be in the stall too long, and if you left the temperature at 225 to 250, it would stay there forever and would truly be a stall. If you do that, your stall could last 6 hours. Who has the time? Cranking up the heat and cooking it even just 25 degrees hotter will be enough to push it through without getting too hot.

At this point, you've spent so much time developing your bark that it's got a firm hold on the meat. We still don't dump the puddles that form. We just leave them on there and let them dry on their own, which they will.

That's what the stall is all about—the meat stops increasing in temperature because it's evaporating a lot of liquid, which keeps the meat cool. However, once the excess fat and liquid are released, when you see that the top of the brisket is dry, it has a good crisp bark, the fat feels soft, and it's internal temp is 170°F, you know that you've made it through the stall.

STAGE 4

300°F

1–2 hours

Now it's time for the final push to render all the top fat. To get there, we go to 300°F after the stall for another 1 to 2 hours. Because most of the liquid has been released, the brisket cooks more quickly. Its internal temperature could go from 170 to 200 in as little as an hour.

What we're aiming for in this stage is for the crusty top bark to feel airy underneath. If you were to push down on the top, it would feel as if there's an air pocket in between the bark and the meat. The bark is like a shell on the meat. There might even be a bit of bubbling up on the bark a bit. This is the good kind of crispy, which is the goal, and this means that the fat is nicely rendered. The internal temperature of the meat will be about 195 to 200°F.

We don't wrap the briskets at any point during the cook. Instead, we leave them exposed the whole time they are in the smoker. This renders the fat most efficiently and creates the best bark. We used to wrap them at 185°F and then place them back in until they reached 200, but once you wrap them, they start to cook fast.

STEP 8: PULL, WRAP, AND REST

Foil
Tallow (page 201)

We pull at 200°F, which is a little undercooked. But as it rests, the temperature will rise. If you're serving it immediately, you can cook it to between 205 and 210. Since we rest ours overnight in the warmer, it's better to go a little under; otherwise it will be overcooked and dried out. With our way, we can serve it to the customer perfectly juicy and tender.

Now, because we're cooking on 1,000-gallon offsets, the high end of the temperature ranges for each stage are the perfect temperatures for us. When you're cooking on a smaller backyard smoker, you will want to aim for the lower temperatures in the range because the meat will be closer to the fire. On a smaller smoker, 275°F will be similar to 300°F on a 1,000-gallon smoker.

When you pull the brisket off the smoker to rest, the outer edges will cool down faster than the middle, so you don't need to worry about them. All that radiant heat is trapped in the center, so as it rests, the center will continue to rise in temperature before cooling, while the edges are already cool. Eventually, the center will catch up with the edges, and it will all be even.

The middle will always feel tighter than the edges, but once the middle has a good amount of tenderness, then you know that the edges are going to be super tender too.

As for the fat, the goal is to not see any white fat on the point under the bark. When we check the brisket to see whether it's ready to pull, we gently pull apart a small slit into the bark on the money bites side opposite the mohawk and look at the fat. If it's a caramel color, then it's rendered. If you see white or yellow, however, it's not rendered enough and it will need to cook longer.

Checking to see whether the fat has rendered.

After pulling, we immediately wrap the briskets. For each brisket, we use two sheets of foil, which are each about three times the length of the brisket. We use two sheets because it's less likely that the foil will break and then leak all the tallow. We started out using butcher paper to wrap our briskets, but the tallow leaked everywhere and there was way more tallow on the floor than on the briskets. So we find that foil does a much better job. Our floors are now cleaner too!

For each brisket, we'll use 1 cup of melted tallow. We pour this in the bottom of the foil in the center, then place the brisket, fat-side up, on top of the tallow.

To wrap, we then bring each side of the foil sheets over the brisket, left and right. Then we wrap the top and bottom portions of the foil over the brisket. While we want it to be enclosed and sealed, we don't seal the foil too tightly because we want the tallow to be able to move around and soften any crisp edges. You want a nice, soft wrap; that way, it will steam up nicely and any crispy parts on the edges or top will soften up too.

Place the brisket on the tallow.

Fold over the foil on one side.

Bring over the other side of the foil.

Bring up the top and bottom pieces of foil.

Tighten all around.

STEPS OF WRAPPING THE BRISKET

Let the brisket rest wrapped on a table inside at room temperature until the internal temperature has dropped to 150°F if you're planning to keep it in a warmer overnight. Let it drop to 140°F if you're going to eat it immediately. This takes about 2 to 2½ hours.

We take the temp in the center of the foil on the top side, just as we've done the entire cook. Be gentle when probing because you don't want to push the probe through the bottom of the foil, which will cause the tallow to leak everywhere. A total mess!

The higher temperature works better if it's going into a warmer because it will be less likely to overcook. Our warmers are set at 140°F, which the brisket will eventually cool down to while it's in there.

We hold our briskets for 12 hours in the warmer. When you start to go past that, the brisket will oxidize more quickly when you cut into it. Oxidation means that the meat will start to go from light brown to gray. It will still taste good, but it won't look as appealing.

Now, we know that most of you won't have a professional-grade warmer, so if you want to hold your brisket, you can do a few things.

One, you can warm up a well-insulated cooler by pouring boiling water into it, closing the lid, and letting the water sit in there for about 20 minutes to warm up the cooler. After this time, pour out the water. Place a heavy towel in the bottom of the cooler and place the brisket on top of it. Close the lid, and the brisket will hold like this for 5 hours or so.

You can also place the brisket in your oven at its lowest temperature. If your oven goes down to 140, set it there. We've seen that most ovens, however, only go down to 170, so you can either wedge the oven door open an inch or leave it in the oven for only 2 to 3 hours.

Some large toaster ovens can be set at 140, so that's another option, though it will only hold one brisket.

STEP 9: CUT

When you're ready to serve your brisket, place it still wrapped in foil on the cutting board. A 10-inch serrated knife is our preferred tool.

Open the foil packet and lift out the brisket, placing it on the cutting board fat-side up. We then pour the juices from the foil over the top of the brisket.

Because we're using so much tallow, it will cut through some of the spices, which is why we tend to almost over-season. You want the seasoning to cut through all that fat!

When you're cutting the brisket, if you look at the bottom, you'll see the grains running from the mohawk to the thick side of the lean. You want to cut against the grain, and since there's always going to be a thicker side of the lean, you're going to start at that corner.

You'll then cut the lean at a slight angle, working your way up the lean until you get to the mohawk. You want the slices to be pencil-thin, but you can go thinner if it's undercooked, and if it's starting to tear because it's overcooked, then you can go a little thicker.

For the cuts, we don't place much pressure while going through the bark so it will stay intact. But once the knife is in the meat, we add more pressure as we saw the knife back and forth. To keep the cuts clean and to keep the meat from shredding all over the board, we finish each slice with the final knife stroke pulled toward us, versus the other side of the meat.

After you've worked your way through the lean and you're at the base of the mohawk, you're now at the point. When you get to the point, you want to rotate the mohawk side away from your cutting hand one turn.

You do this because the grains in the point run in the opposite direction than those in the lean, and you still want to cut against the grain.

You're then going to cut into the point from the money bites side to the mohawk. As you can see, the mohawk is an important point of reference for cutting meat, so be sure to recognize where it is.

The first slice on the point is the best slice on the entire brisket. But first, remember the deckle fat that we removed when we were trimming the brisket? Some of that fat is still there since it was doing its job of protecting the point.

Our first cut is a parallel cut under the meat to get that fat out. We throw it away since it's nothing but fat. Everyone will complain, but trust us, it's not anything you want to eat.

Now then, on to the good stuff. The first cut you make on the point, which is covered in bark, are the burnt ends. We cut them into small cubes to share with our customers, though as the cook, you're welcome to pop some into your mouth. Sit back and savor that bite! It will be smoky, juicy, and a big beefy flavor bomb!

When we offer them to our customers, they always end up ordering more brisket, even if they were planning to get only a few ribs and turkey! This is why it's called the money bites. Many will say the burnt ends are the best cut on the entire brisket.

As we slice through the point, we're cutting these slices thicker than the lean, almost two pencils wide. As we did for the lean, we barely add any pressure when going through the bark and then add more as we cut through the meat. If the point looks undercooked, then you'll slice it thinner. And if it looks overcooked, you can slice it thicker.

When you reach the mohawk, stop cutting. We don't make clean slices from the mohawk side of the point; instead, it's going to be chopped beef. To do this, first flip the remaining point and place it meat-side down on the board. Now cut down into the mohawk in the center. The lean portion of the brisket runs the entire length, with the fattier point on.

After you've cut into the mohawk, you'll see a thick band of fat running between the point side and the lean side. This fat may be well rendered, but since this is the hardest fat to render in the entire brisket, it will sometimes still be white. That's okay because you're going to cut it out and discard it. This leaves two pieces of meat on the board, the top of the mohawk and the lean that runs underneath.

You can serve the topside portion of the mohawk two ways. If it's soft, you can cut it into cubes for burnt ends. If it's crispy, you can use it for chopped beef. The lean piece is used only for chopped beef. It should be nice and tender, and you can either pull it apart with your hands or roughly chop it with the knife. Then lightly sauce it and serve it. (For our chopped beef sandwich recipe, see page 215).

If you're not going to serve the whole brisket immediately, we recommend cutting only what you are eating, then wrapping the remaining portion in foil with some tallow. You can keep it refrigerated for up to 5 days and then reheat it in your oven in the foil-wrapped package at 200°F.

You'll cook it until the meat probes at a temperature of 140°F, which will vary depending on the size. When serving, remove it from the foil and pour the tallow and juices over the meat before cutting. The meat that was exposed to air will be oxidized and a dull, brown color. We recommend cutting this portion off and discarding it before serving the rest.

If you have a whole brisket that you want to store, you'll keep it refrigerated, wrapped in foil with the

Slicing the brisket.

The point separated from the lean.

Slicing the point.

tallow. You'll also reheat it in the oven at 200°F. A whole brisket will take about 2 to 3 hours to be ready. Jonny swears that reheated whole briskets can often taste better than fresh!

STEP 10: QUALITY CONTROL

Every slice will be different, which is the challenge when serving brisket. Your goal is to serve it as soon as you cut into it. This prevents it from drying out and oxidizing. Brisket is at its best when it's cut to order, which is why there are long lines at barbecue restaurants. Every customer is receiving a freshly prepared tray. We carve to order.

When you assess your slices from the lean, you want the layer of fat to have a nice brownish color, which is a sign that you've achieved your goal of fully rendering the fat. You don't want to see any white or yellow fat, which would be unrendered. This is the ideal, though if you haven't fully rendered all the fat, that's okay too.

As you hold your slice, it should be pliable and glistening, not stiff and dry. When you take a bite, you want the texture to be tender and juicy. Even if there's a slight chew, it's still succulent and you don't need to struggle to get your teeth into the meat. The flavor should be smoky, beefy, peppery, and salty, all in good balance and not overpowering. Any other seasonings you added to the top layer may be present too.

Now on to the point. You want the top fat to be brown and not white or yellow. Ideally, the bark will fade right into the meat, with no visible line of fat. This means it's been rendered perfectly. The grains should be intact and not mushy. If they're mushy then it's been overcooked.

If you undercooked it, then you'll see more fat between the grains, which is a sign that that fat hasn't rendered. The point is super marbled, and your goal is to balance cooking it to where the fat is rendered but the grains are still intact.

One thing about the point is that it's two muscles, and you'll see this as you cut each slice. On the bottom will be the lean, and above that will be the point. Some people will only eat the top, fatty portion and discard the lean. But the lean is also tender and juicy, so give it a try too!

BRISKET, SHORT VERSION

1 packer-cut choice brisket, 10–15 pounds
Coarse black pepper
Table salt
Seasoned salt (page 200)
Melted tallow

Large cutting board
6-inch boning knife
Spray bottle filled with warm water
Instant-read thermometer
1-cup measuring cup
Foil
10-inch serrated knife

Start a bundle fire in your smoker while you prepare for the cook so you can build your coal bed.

Trim your brisket.

Starting on the back side of the brisket, spray with warm water. To season, do one pass with the pepper and one pass with the table salt.

Flip over the brisket and then spray the water over the meat. Evenly shake the pepper over the rack, making 1 pass, then follow with the table salt and then seasoned salt.

Place the brisket on the smoker, then build a log-cabin fire large enough to get the smoker up to 200 to 225°F. After the logs burn down and you have a coal bed, continue to build your fires.

For the first two hours, strive for a consistent 200 to 225°F on the smoker. For the next two hours, strive for 225 to 250°F.

At this point, the brisket will be in the stall. There may be puddles on the lean, and the meat will probably hover at an internal temperature of around 165°F for several hours. To get the brisket beyond this point, now push the fire temperature to between 250 and 275°F.

When the brisket is no longer in the stall and its temperature is rising again, give it the final push to render the top fat by building fires in the 275-to-300°F range.

When the brisket probes like butter and has an internal temperature around 200°F, it's time to pull the brisket.

Pull out a sheet of foil that is three brisket lengths, place a scoop of melted tallow in the center, and place the brisket on top of the tallow. Wrap the brisket, and let it rest until its internal temperature is 150°F. Serve or place in a warmer until ready to serve. Serve warm.

BEEF RIBS

Beef plate ribs, which are also known as dino ribs or short ribs (though they're long in length), are a relatively new star of the Texas barbecue tray. The exact originator is not known, but Louis Mueller Barbecue in Taylor, Texas, is the place that made them famous and a destination-worthy item. To this day, it's what people talk about ordering when they visit this iconic spot.

Their appeal is no surprise since a beef rib is all the juicy, fatty portions of the brisket contained in one meaty package. If you're inclined to order fatty brisket, or you're a fan of rich and succulent beef, then you'll love beef ribs.

We don't fuss with ours too much. Instead, we give them a slight trim, season them, and throw them on the fire. The entire process takes little effort and they're a forgiving cut, so they're hard to bungle. Instead, the ribs do all the work for you with their marbled meat and thick, fatty structure. Each bite will be tender, juicy, and beefy. You can't go wrong.

Right now, we are not offering beef ribs on our menu, mainly because they're too popular. That may sound crazy, but because we could smoke only a few for each service, they sold out quickly and customers would get upset with us when they were gone. While we also miss them, it was easier for us to remove them from the menu than to keep disappointing those who couldn't order them.

However, if you miss our beef ribs, here is our recipe to make them at home. They're super chill, and you will be delighted with the results. You just cook them until they're super, super tender, and they're good to go. It's an excellent gateway meat, and you will feel like such a rock star when you pull this luscious slab of meat and bone off the smoker. Your guests will thank you too.

STEP 1: TOOLS

Large cutting board
10-inch chef's knife
Serrated knife
Foil

STEP 2: MEAT

1 4-pound (1.81-kilogram) rack of choice plate ribs, with 3 or 4 bones

We use beef plate ribs that come with three long bones. Our ribs are choice grade, and we find this is the perfect balance between fat and meat. If you want to splurge, you could go with prime or Wagyu, but choice is more economical and delivers as much bang as the more expensive cuts. Also, with the more expensive cuts you're getting more fat that needs to be rendered, which will call for a longer, hotter cook. It's already a fatty cut of meat and even more fat is a bit much, we believe.

Beef plate ribs are easy to find here in Texas. When cooking at home, we get ours at HEB grocery store, though Costco and Walmart also sell them. If you're not in Texas, the latter two will most likely have the cut, or you can ask your local grocery store's butcher or an independent butcher to assist.

When shopping for beef ribs, we look for a solid fat cap on top and meat that is thick and decently marbled. Sometimes, all the available beef ribs will have already been trimmed on top and there won't be much fat. This is okay. The ones we would receive at the restaurant would often not have much of a fat cap either. If your fire management is dialed in and there's plenty of marbled meat, the ribs will still come out succulent.

STEP 3: TRIMMING

You don't have to trim beef ribs too much. If there's a heavy fat cap, we like to trim it down a little bit, just because we don't think beef ribs need the fat cap as much as brisket. But we don't want to take it all down because it does taste really good.

To begin, we place the rack on the cutting board, meat-side down, and then score the membrane on the back side with the knife in the shape of an X. We don't remove the membrane because it will eventually melt away as it cooks and won't affect your eating experience. It also helps keep the rack stay together as it cooks, so we see it as an advantage.

After we score the back, we flip the rack and look at the top. If there's a blanket of solid, thick fat, you'll want to trim that down so that it's ¼-inch thick. We do this by making gentle cuts with the boning knife across the fat cap.

Usually, however, the cap has already been trimmed, and if this is the case, you can simply leave what is there on the rack. If there is a patch that's more than ¼-inch thick, you can trim it so the fat will render properly.

Last, we round off the corners so they don't catch as much heat and crisp up and burn. If you want to save the trim for chili or sausage, you may.

STEP 4: SEASONING

Prepared yellow mustard
Water
Seasoned salt (page 200)
Coarse black pepper

First, stir together one part mustard with one part water. You'll need only a couple of teaspoons total for each rack, so keep that in mind. This will be your binder.

For seasoning, we start on the membrane side. Because the membrane will melt away as the rack cooks, you don't need any seasoning on this side. Instead, we do it just for looks and color.

To season, we hold the shaker at eye level and then, starting at one end, sprinkle the seasoned salt evenly across the rack until we reach the other end. We're not putting pepper on this side because it will just fall off and that's a waste.

Next, we flip over the rack. For the meatier side,

we apply our binder. Spread the binder evenly over the meat. We use our hands, taking care to use one hand for handling the raw meat and the other hand for handling binders and seasoning bottles.

Next, we do two passes of black pepper, giving the meat a good covering. Go through and apply to any bald spots you may have missed, and where there's fat, make sure there's a good coating for extra color. Hit all the sides of the rack with the pepper too. As we've explained, pepper attracts smoke, and this will ensure that the rack has a hearty, flavorful bark.

Now, we generously apply the seasoned salt, doing two passes. Again, hit any spots you may have missed, as well as the sides. We go a little heavier on the salt with these guys so that each bite will be intensely flavorful from smoke, meat, salt, and pepper.

After it's been seasoned, we pat the seasoning into the meat with our hands. To do this, we gently place our hand on the meat, lightly pressing into the spices, and then lift. Don't move your hand around on top of the rack because this will move the salt and pepper around and disrupt your perfectly balanced seasoning! Instead, just place your hand down and then pull it straight up, and again, down and up on repeat until the seasoning is pressed into the meat.

STEP 5: PLACEMENT ON THE SMOKER

After the rack has been seasoned, we place it on the smoker's grates meat-side up, with the rack perpendicular to the firebox. A rack is positioned with the bones running parallel to the sides of the smoker and the thicker end of the meat side facing the fire. If you're doing more than one rack, position them about an inch apart.

STEP 6: FIRE AND SMOKE

We place the ribs on the smoker cold. The first hour in, we're trying to build our coal bed and hit the beef ribs with lots of black, dirty smoke so they will have plenty of flavor and color. For the initial fire, you can build a log-cabin-style fire or a bundle fire (for more detail, see chapter 5); it's your choice. The advantage of the bundle fire is that it produces more smoke, and if you're looking for a smokier rack, this is the way to go since the cook isn't too long.

While ultimately we want the smoker to reach 300°F, we start slowly. In the first hour, yours may rise only to between 250 and 275°F, which is fine. You want to be gentle with the heat so the beef ribs don't get singed. While each smoker is different, for a 90-gallon offset, we'd start with three full logs (or six splits) for the initial burn.

For this first fire, open the damper all the way. Once the fire is lit, close the door almost all the way, leaving it cracked open about an inch. This will pull the smoke through the chamber and allow the wood to burn down and form your bed of coals.

After an hour or so, ideally your smoker will be up to about 300°F. If it's not, don't worry about it too much—it will get there! By this time, the logs will be burnt. With your shovel, break the burnt logs down. Now you have a coal bed.

Build your next fire in a bundle style. We also close the damper halfway. This locks in the heat and helps the fat to render more quickly. For the next 4 or 5 hours, you'll be breaking down and rebuilding fires every half hour or so (a bundle for more smoke, cabin style for less).

Be sure to clean out the ashes from the firebox if there's too much accumulation along the way because you don't want the logs to rise too high. Shoot for a smoker temperature of 300°F during the rest of the cook.

STEP 7: TIME AND TEMPERATURE

The target temperature for a rack of ribs is 200 to 210°F, and it will usually take from 6 to 8 hours to reach this point, depending on the size of your smoker.

Along the way, here is what to expect as it cooks. For the first hour, the ribs will be wet on top. Over the next hour or two, you'll begin to see the bark forming. The top will lose its glossy moisture and start to dry. As the ribs continue to cook, the bark will become thick and crisp, and the meat will begin to shrink from the bones.

When the rack has a thick, solid bark and the bones are becoming more pronounced, about 5 hours into the cook, we start probing it with the thermometer to check for doneness. We probe the rack in its center all the way between the bones. The probe will slide in like it's going into room-temperature butter when the rack is done. The temperature will be between 200 and 210°F.

When you believe a rack is ready to pull, another way to make sure it's done is the bend test. Lift the rack up (with covered hands), holding it on each side, and if you can gently bend it, the rack is done.

Sometimes a bone may fall off the rack, and while this isn't ideal, it's also not the end of the world. Don't worry! Beef ribs are very, very forgiving!

Your ribs are now ready to be pulled and wrapped.

STEP 8: PULL, WRAP, AND REST

Foil
Tallow (page 201)

For wrapping the ribs, pull out a 2-foot-long sheet of foil. Scoop into the center of the foil ½ cup of tallow.

Place the rack on top of the tallow, meat-side up. While it doesn't matter too much which way the bones are facing, we find that you'll have less chance of the packet ripping if the long side of the end bone is facing you.

After admiring your beautiful rack, it's time to wrap. Start on the left side and lift the foil over the rack. Do the same on the right side.

Lift the bottom portion of the foil, closest to you, then fold the top side of the foil across the rack. Tighten the packet along the sides until the rack is contained.

All the folds will be on top, and this is how you want to keep the rack positioned as it rests. This will keep the tallow inside as it melts.

Now that the ribs are wrapped, let them rest at room temperature until they're 140°F, about 1½ hours. Then you can either unwrap them and eat them, or place them in a warmer or prepared cooler.

Beef ribs can keep for up to 12 hours, but it's ideal to keep the hold to around 6 hours, as they can begin to lose their integrity the longer they hold.

STEP 9: CUT

Your ribs are ready to serve! Grab your serrated knife, and let's cut these beautiful babies.

First, unwrap the ribs and place the rack on the cutting board, meat-side up. Shake out the tallow and the juices from the foil on top of the meat.

Unlike cutting other meats, the technique for ribs is the same as cutting a slice of bread from a loaf. Take the knife, find the spot in between the bones where it's only meat, and slice. You'll make two cuts and have three ribs. (For a four-bone rack, you'll make three cuts.)

The center rib will most likely be the money shot, as it's usually the thickest, tallest rib. Sometimes one or both of the end ribs may be a bit shrunken and less uniform in shape than the center, though they will still taste delicious.

STEP 10: QUALITY CONTROL

Let's look at your rib. Hopefully, the meat will sit in the center of the flat, long bone, and the bark will be crisp and thick but not burnt.

The interior of the meat will be a glossy light brown with a gentle red smoke ring along the edges. All the fat, both under the bark and inside the rib, will be rendered. There will be no white patches. If you give the rib a gentle squeeze, juices will run.

Take a bite. You want it to be tender, juicy, almost melting into your mouth. The bark will have a slight crunch and be salty and peppery, but just enough, not too much. The meat will easily pull apart.

How's the flavor? Do you taste smoke? How are the levels of salt and pepper? Make notes about what you would do next time, but also enjoy this moment. You have successfully cooked a succulent rack of beef ribs.

BEEF RIBS, SHORT VERSION

1 4-pound (1.81-kilogram) rack of choice plate ribs, with 3 or 4 bones
1 teaspoon water
1 teaspoon prepared yellow mustard
Seasoned salt (page 200)
Coarse black pepper
Tallow (page 201)

Cutting board
10-inch chef's knife
Shakers
Instant-read meat thermometer
Foil
Serrated knife

Score the membrane on the back of the rack with an X. Then, lightly trim the corners so they are rounded and aerodynamic.

Mix the mustard and water to form a binder. Starting on the back of the rack, shake on the seasoned salt evenly, making one pass down the rack.

Flip the rack and then evenly rub the binder over the meat. Evenly shake the pepper over the rack, making two passes. Hit the sides with the pepper too.

Next, make two passes with the seasoned salt on top, also hitting the sides.

Place the ribs meat-side up on the smoker, and build and light a bundle fire large enough to get the smoker up to 250°F. After the logs burn down and you have a coal bed, continue to build your fires, using a bundle for a smokier cook and cabin style for a less smoky cook, aiming for 300°F.

When the meat has a thick, black bark, has pulled away from the bones, bends easily, and has an internal temperature of about 200°F, pull the rack.

Tear off a 2-foot-long sheet of foil. Place ½ cup of tallow in the center of the foil. Lay the rack on top of the tallow, meat-side up. Lift the edges of the foil up and around the rack, squeezing the edges so a tight packet is formed.

Let the ribs rest for 1½ hours or until they're 140°F. Serve warm or keep in a warmer for up to 12 hours.

PORK RIBS

"Ribs are weird," said Lane. He was poking the racks he had been smoking since around 2:00 a.m., and as the sun was peeking over the horizon, it wasn't clear whether he was bonkers with exhaustion or just getting into his groove.

One of the apprentices asked him to elaborate. Lane laughed and said it was hard to explain, but when it came to ribs, there were no set rules. He handed the thermometer to her and asked her to slide it into the rack in between the bones. She did and noticed that the temperature was 175°F. He then told her to poke it into the bones, and the temperature was 10°F warmer.

"It's hard to go by temperature with ribs," he explained, "because all the bones throw you off." Instead, he pointed at the golden sheen on top of the ribs and said that was rendered fat. Visually, when the ribs turn a deep red that looks like they've been glazed with gold, they're on their way to being done. Ribs can be tricky, but if you know the signs, you can produce excellent ribs every time.

While everyone at the restaurant rotates doing the rib shift, Lane feels especially passionate about this job. He grew up eating his father's smoked ribs, which even though they were glazed in Dr Pepper, Lane had always felt could be improved. It wasn't until he began working the rib shift at Freedmen's that he figured out how to prepare ribs that he could enjoy.

That said, Lane will be quick to tell you that we're all super picky about ribs, probably to the point that we don't even *like* ribs. But we do like our ribs at Goldee's. They are truly the best. You may be asking, what makes them so special? Well, first, they're tender and firm. Our cooking is all about balance, and our pork ribs' flavor profile is no different: They are equal parts tangy and sweet.

We also try to blast tons of smoke on the ribs in the relatively short time they take to cook. Because we only use post oak, which is a mild wood, we build smoky fires for our ribs and don't wrap them until they're done cooking. This not only hits them with the maximum amount of smoke but also creates a firm bark.

When we wrap the ribs, we hit them with our rib glaze, which is only one note of many and not the dominant player. The glaze is a thin sauce, so it's not overpowering. It blends with the whole bite, which is porky, smoky, salty, a little sweet, and a little tangy. You can't put our ribs into one category. Instead, they're a harmonious blend of all the things we want to see in ribs.

Sure, Lane likes to say that ribs are weird. But this is Texas, where weird is a compliment and our weird ribs are good!

STEP 1: TOOLS

Large cutting board
10-inch chef's knife
Foil
Squirt bottle

You will need a cutting board to trim the ribs, and since you're going to be cutting thick cartilage, you'll want a heavier knife. We use foil to wrap the ribs when they're done, and the squirt bottle will be filled with rib glaze, which we paint onto the foil before we set down the ribs for their wrap and rest.

STEP 2: MEAT

Full rack spare pork spareribs, about 5 pounds (2.27 kilograms)

At the restaurant, we use Duroc pork. These pigs produce ribs with superior fat marbling, which not only attracts lots of smoky flavors but also yields a juicier, meatier rib. We buy the full rack spare so we can trim it down to our preferred shape, saving the trim for our Kennedale pork hash.

When you are looking to buy ribs at the store, get the full spares. Large grocery stores typically carry them, but if you only see precut ribs such as baby back or St. Louis cut, ask the butcher if they have full spares in the back.

Look for ribs that feel plush when you squeeze them and have a good balance of red meat and marbling. If they're frozen, get the thickest racks. This will ensure that they cook up nice and juicy.

Also, if you can see any bones poking through on the meat side, pass. You can't eat the bones, and you don't want to pay for that! Finally, if you have a choice in sizes, always get the largest. They're meatier, and if you're investing all that time to cook them, you might as well have a satisfying bite at the end.

STEP 3: TRIMMING

The reason why we want you to get a full spare instead of the pretrimmed St. Louis cut is that we want you to have more meat. Likewise, by trimming the rack yourself, you will not only get a larger rib but also have trims that you can do fun things with, like make our Kennedale pork hash (page 212) and pork stock (page 201).

What is a St. Louis cut? Well, it's a flat rack of spareribs (as opposed to curved baby backs, which are closer to the spine, as the name implies, rather than the belly, as spareribs are) that has been trimmed down to a rectangular shape, with the chine bone and the tips removed. While we also remove the chine bone and shape the rack, we do it less aggressively, so each rib is longer and meatier.

Because we save what we trim to avoid waste, we keep one tub for the meat we use in our Kennedale pork hash and one tub for the bones used in pork stock. If you wish to use the trim for these recipes, do the same. We also use a chef's knife instead of a boning knife to trim the pork ribs. The chef's knife is thicker and sturdier, and it can cut through the cartilage more easily.

After you remove the rack of ribs from its packaging, first look at the back. This is the side with a full membrane running across the bones. We don't remove the membrane because it will shrink while cooking and will also help hold the rack together. You may remove it if you wish, though. Lane says that taking the membrane off pork ribs might be beneficial in some smokers.

On the back side, however, you will see a thin flap of pork meat that's running at an angle. This piece of meat is known as the skirt. While it's tasty, its presence will prevent the rack from cooking as evenly as it could, so we remove it. This trim will be used for our Kennedale pork hash.

The next cut is the removal of the top bone, which is known as the chine bone. You can identify it and cut it more easily with the rack bone-side up, so leaving the rack this way, find the bone, which runs at an angle across the corner on the thicker end of the ribs.

Following the bone with your knife, press down and make a firm cut so you can remove it. If your knife is sharp, with a bit of pressure, the bone will most likely come off easily. If you're into sound effects, you will notice a satisfying crunch as your knife moves through the cartilage and bone.

Since this will be your first bone cut, here's how to deal with the cuts that have both bone and meat. We trim the meat off the bone and place that in our Kennedale pork hash tub. The bone itself goes into the pork stock tub. But you could use the whole bone with the meat on it for stock too. Either one is fine.

While still on the back side, look at the narrow end of the rack. There is often a thin flap of meat with a bone so small that it would fall out during the cook. We don't want to keep this, so to remove it, feel where that little bone ends, then cut it and the flap of meat off the rack. This will leave a nice, meaty bone to begin the rack. Last, if there are any hanging bits of fat on the back, trim those too.

Now flip the rack over. On the top of the rack, run your knife along the length, evening out the shape of the rack so it's in a more aerodynamic line. If there's an excess of top fat on the meat side, usually by where the chine bone was, you can trim that down. Last, we round out the corners and edges so it will cook more evenly and nothing will burn.

STEP 4: SEASONING

Prepared yellow mustard
Water
Coarse black pepper
Seasoned salt (page 200)

First, stir together one part mustard with one part water. You'll need only a couple of teaspoons total for each rack, so keep that in mind. This will be your binder.

For our seasoning, we begin on the back side of the ribs. We don't do too much on this side except give it two passes of seasoned salt. For this, we hold the shaker at eye level and then, starting at one end, sprinkle the seasoned salt evenly across the rack until we reach the other end, then repeat. We're not putting pepper on this side because it will just fall off and that's a waste.

Next, we flip over the rack. For the meatier side, we apply our binder. Spread the binder evenly over the meat. We use our hands, taking care to use one hand for handling the raw meat and the other hand for handling binders and seasoning bottles.

After the binder is on the rack, we do two passes of black pepper, giving the meat a good covering. Go through and apply to any bald spots you may have missed, and where there's fat, make sure there's a good coating for extra color.

Now, we generously apply the seasoned salt, doing one pass. Again, hit any spots you may have missed.

STEP 5: PLACEMENT ON THE SMOKER

We place the racks on the grate meat-side up, with the rack perpendicular to the firebox. The racks are positioned with the thicker-bone end closest to the wall and the thinner-bone side next to the door. The door side is cooler, and we place the more delicate side toward it so it has less opportunity to burn.

If you're doing more than one rack, position them about an inch apart. After you place the ribs on the grate, place your hands on each end, thick and thin, and then gently smash the rack inward so it's plumper and fuller. This will also help keep it from getting too crispy as it cooks.

STEP 6: FIRE AND SMOKE

We place the ribs on the smoker cold. For the first hour, we're trying to build our coal bed and hit the ribs with smoke. For the initial fire, you can build a log-cabin-style fire or a bundle fire (for more detail, see chapter 5); it's your choice. The advantage of the bundle fire is that it produces more smoke, and if you're looking for a smokier rack, this is the way to go since the cook isn't too long.

While ultimately we want the smoker to reach 275°F, we start slow. In the first hour, yours may rise only to 250°F, which is fine. You want to be gentle with the heat so the ribs don't get singed. While each smoker is different, for a 90-gallon offset, we'd start with two full logs (or four splits) for the initial burn.

For this first fire, open the damper all the way. Once the fire is lit, close the door almost all the way, leaving it cracked open about an inch. This will pull the smoke through the chamber and allow the wood to burn down and form your bed of coals.

After an hour or so, ideally your smoker will be up to about 250°F. If it's not, don't worry about it too much—it will get there! At this time, the logs will be burnt. With your shovel, break the burnt logs down. Now you have a coal bed.

Build your next fire in either a log-cabin style or bundle. Ribs are thin, and if you don't want them overly smoky, stick with a log-cabin build. We'll also close the damper halfway. This locks in the heat and helps the fat to render more quickly. For the next 4 or 5 hours, you'll be simply breaking down and rebuilding your fires every half hour or so.

Be sure to clean out the ashes from the firebox if there's too much accumulation along the way because you don't want the logs to rise too high. Shoot for a smoker temperature of 275°F during the rest of the cook.

STEP 7: TIME AND TEMPERATURE

The target temperature for a rack of ribs is 190 to 200°F, and it will usually take from 4 to 6 hours to reach this point.

Along the way, here is what to expect as it cooks. For the first hour or so, the ribs will be wet on top. Over the next hour or two, you'll begin to see golden pools form on top of the rack, which is the fat rendering. Starting at the edges, the meat will begin to darken and become glossy.

The meat will also start to dry, and the bark will begin to set. Go ahead and touch them—does the meat feel dry? That's good! They're coming along quite nicely. After several more hours, about 4 or so hours into the cook, the ribs will take on a deeper red hue.

At Goldee's, we strive to get them darker since we're going to wrap them with our rib glaze, which will not only tone down the color a bit but also soften the meat. You'll also see the gold spots on top, which is the rendered fat.

The ribs will be done anywhere from 4½ hours to 6 hours into the cook, depending on your fires, the size of the rack, and the outside temperatures. When you rebuild your fires, open the chamber door and check their progress. You'll see them grow darker in color. You can also check the temperature in the center of the rack, where it's thickest.

(If you're worried about opening the chamber door and losing heat, simply throw on another log, as Lane does. But it's a myth that you need to keep the chamber door shut. Our eyes and hands are our best tools for gauging where the meat is during the cooking process. Jonny says, "Look and cook!")

Again, your goal internal temperature for the rack is 190°F. You'll also know they're done when the probe slides in like butter and the ribs are a rich, dark red. When you pick up the rack, it should bend nicely. They're now ready to be wrapped. While they rest, they'll continue to rise in temperature until they're about 200°F before cooling.

STEP 8: PULL, WRAP, AND REST

To wrap the rips, pull out a 3-foot-long sheet of foil. Fill the squeeze bottle with the rib glaze (page 193). In the center of the foil, squirt the rib glaze into a rectangle the same width and height as the rack. Be generous with your squirts. It's okay if it's not perfect, though err on the side of doing too much versus too little.

After admiring the way your ribs look and feel, gently place them meat-side down on top of the glaze. Feel along the short end of the rack. Sometimes there will be a tiny bone hanging down—pull this off. If there's any meat attached, feel free to nibble and get a pitmaster's treat!

To wrap, start on the right side and bring that sheet of foil over the ribs. Then, bring the left side over the ribs. Fold the top and bottom edges up and over the ribs, then gently press along the edges to form a tight seal.

Saucing the ribs.

Pull over one side of the foil.

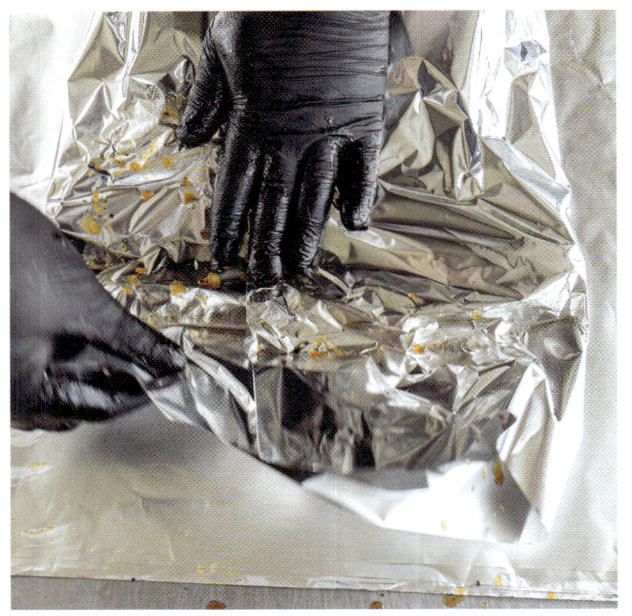

Bring over the other side of foil.

Tighten all around.

STEPS OF WRAPPING RIBS

If the foil packet rips when you're wrapping because of a sharp bone, just start over. You don't want a ripped packet because the sauce will leak and the ribs will dry out. It happens to the best of us, and it's nothing to be concerned about. Blame the foil, not the cook!

After the ribs are wrapped, let them rest at room temperature until their internal temperature is 140°F, about 1½ hours. Now you can either unwrap them and eat them, or place them in a warmer or prepared cooler. Ribs can keep for up to 12 hours, but it's ideal to limit the hold to around 6 hours, as they can begin to lose their integrity the longer the hold.

STEP 9: CUTTING

Ribs can be tricky. It's not a straight slice because the bones are set at a slight angle. When they're first beginning, some people even flip the rack over and cut from the back, since the bones are more pronounced there. If you choose to do this, that's totally fine. Some of the sauce and bark will be left on the cutting board, but not enough to affect the flavor. And you'll have even ribs, which may be important to you.

First we place the wrapped ribs fold-side up on the cutting board, then open the foil. We flip the ribs out of the packet so that they land meat-side up on the board. Finally, we pull away the foil and then shake the sheet over the ribs so any remaining sauce will land on them.

Looking at the rack, you'll notice that the bones are arranged in a fan shape. Place the knife in your dominant hand, and with your other hand gently pat the top of the rack so you can gauge the placement of the bones. You want to make your cuts in the center between two bones so each bone will form a separate rib with plenty of meat.

Start cutting at one end (the end will probably be determined by your dominant hand), and as you make each cut, you'll notice that your knife slowly shifts its angle.

For example, for the first cut, your knife may have a 70-degree angle. But as you work your way down the rack, you'll see that it shifts closer to a 90-degree angle with each cut. And by the time you're in the center of the rack, it will be close to pointing straight up.

Go slowly until you get a feel for the rack. It's fine if you hit the bones. We still do sometimes too! Just lift the knife and reposition it. The rib will still be tasty no matter how pretty the cut is.

STEP 10: QUALITY CONTROL

Okay, this is the moment you've been waiting for—it's time to eat! But first, let's look at your rib. Hopefully, it's dark red with a slight sheen, and it's still attached to the bone. If you hold it up and give it a gentle squeeze, juices will start to run.

Take a bite. You want it to be tender but with a slight hint of chew. You don't want to be fighting with the texture, but you also don't want it to be mushy. How's the flavor? Do you taste smoke? Is it sweet and tangy? How are the levels of salt and pepper?

Think about each bite, give yourself praise for all that makes you happy, and take notes about what you can improve next time. Most importantly, enjoy what you've made! We still criticize each of our cooks so we can improve, but at the same time, we also love what we make. And you have just smoked a weirdly beautiful rack of ribs.

PORK RIBS, SHORT VERSION

1 5-pound (2.27-kilogram) rack of pork spareribs
1 teaspoon yellow prepared mustard
1 teaspoon water
Seasoned salt (page 200)
Coarse black pepper
Rib glaze (page 193)

Cutting board
10-inch chef's knife
Shakers
Instant-read meat thermometer
Squeeze bottle
Foil

Trim your rack of ribs. Then, mix the mustard and water to form a binder. Starting on the back of the rack, shake out the seasoned salt evenly, making two passes down the rack.

Flip the rack over and then evenly rub the binder over the meat. Evenly shake the pepper over the rack, making two passes, then follow with the seasoned salt.

Place the ribs on the smoker, and build and light a bundle fire large enough to get the smoker up to 250°F. After the logs burn down and you have a coal bed, continue to build your fires, choosing a bundle for a smokier cook and cabin style for a less smoky cook, aiming for 275°F.

When the ribs are deep red with golden spots of rendered fat, easily bend, and have an internal temperature of about 190°F, pull the rack.

Tear off a 3-foot-long sheet of foil. Pour the rib glaze in the squeeze bottle, then squirt a rack-size layer of glaze onto the foil. Gently place the rack meat-side down into this puddle, then fold the foil over the rack. Let it rest for 1½ hours or until it's 140°F. Serve warm.

PORK BELLY

Jonny had a vision. "I'm going to make the best pork belly in the world," he said. "I'm going to make pork belly as beloved as brisket." If the response to our sliced pork belly is any indication, he may have achieved his goal. People love pork belly.

It's a later addition that was designed to fill the hole that was left when we decided to remove beef ribs (page 149) from the tray. We couldn't keep up with the demand for beef ribs, and they sold out fast. This led to disappointed customers. We were tired of people getting annoyed with us, so we just got rid of them altogether.

While pork belly neither tastes nor resembles a slab of juicy beef on a bone, Jonny thought he could achieve a similar effect. Most Texas barbecue places offer pork belly as a "burnt end" dish. This means that they cut the belly into cubes, smoke them until crisp, and then heavily sauce the meat. It's a candied dish.

Jonny's idea, however, was to play up pork belly's natural sweetness. To do this, he seasoned the bellies only with salt. He cut his full bellies into three manageable cuts that would render and cook quickly yet could still be sliced. That last goal was key, since Jonny wanted to serve pork belly like a brisket, with slices equally as rich, tender, and juicy.

Beef ribs are a rich dish, and so is pork belly. Anyone who eats Goldee's pork belly will feel that wave of luxury that comes from such unsullied rendered fat. "It tastes like uncured bacon," Jonny says, and who doesn't like bacon?

Lane came up with a peach glaze to serve on the side, if you're so inclined. And now almost everyone orders pork belly for their tray. Thankfully, there's plenty to go around.

STEP 1: TOOLS

Cutting board
Boning knife
Thermometer

STEP 2: MEAT

1 10-to-12-pound (4.5-to-5.4-kilogram) boneless, skinless pork belly
Coarse black pepper
Seasoned salt (page 200)
Peach glaze (page 194)

At the restaurant, we use whole boneless bellies, which run about 10 to 12 pounds. We're looking for bellies that have a full white fat cap and decent marbling in the meat underneath.

If your store doesn't offer the full belly, ask if they offer a cut belly, which is usually about 2 to 3 pounds. That will work too.

STEP 3: TRIMMING

If using a full boneless belly, trim the pork belly lengthwise into four equally sized portions. If you're using only a portion of a boneless belly, don't divide it into pieces any less than 3 inches wide; they're extremely fatty and will shrink.

After you've cut off your portions, take your knife and round off the corners of each portion. And that's it for trimming!

STEP 4: SEASONING

When we started cooking pork bellies, our only seasoning was table salt. We were pleased with the results, but after time we decided to add a few more layers of flavor, which we now achieve by using our seasoned salt and black pepper. These seasonings also add color.

The pork bellies are extremely sticky, so we don't use a binder. We start on the back, or meaty, side and give the meat one pass of the seasoned salt.

Pork bellies.

Trimming the pork bellies.

Trimmed pork bellies.

Seasoning the bellies with pepper.

Seasoning the bellies with seasoned salt.

We then flip over the belly and do one even pass of black pepper over the fat. Then we do one even pass with the seasoned salt. We gently pat the seasoned salt on the fat cap, and then they're ready to go. We don't do anything with the sides.

Don't overseason the belly because it will shrink and become too salty. A standard pass—not too light, not too heavy—on the front and back sides will be plenty.

STEP 5: PLACEMENT ON THE SMOKER

After we've portioned out the bellies, we place them on the smoker. We position them far from the fire, with the grained meat side facing the fire. To identify the grained meat side, find the side that looks like bacon with lines of fat running lengthwise across the cut of meat.

STEP 6: FIRE AND SMOKE

We place the pork belly on the smoker immediately after seasoning. For our first fire, we start with a bundle fire (for more detail, see chapter 5). Bellies cook quickly, and we want to hit them with as much flavor as possible.

While ultimately we want the smoker to reach 275°F, we start slow. In the first hour, yours may rise only to 250°F, which is fine. You want to be gentle with the heat so the belly doesn't get singed. While each smoker is different, for a 90-gallon offset, we'd start with two full logs (or four splits) for the initial burn.

For this first fire, open the damper all the way. Once the fire is lit, close the door almost all the way, leaving it cracked open about an inch. This will pull the smoke through the chamber and allow the wood to burn down and form your bed of coals.

After an hour or so, ideally your smoker will be up to about 250°F. If it's not, don't worry about it too much—it will get there! At this time, the logs will be burnt. With your shovel, break the burnt logs down. Now you have a coal bed.

Build your next fire in a log cabin style or bundle; it's your choice. Lane recommends going with a bundle fire the entire cook if it's the only meat on the smoker. But if you're cooking it with other items that you don't want to get as much smoke, you can do a log cabin style instead.

We also close the damper halfway. This locks in the heat. For the next 3 to 4 hours, you'll be simply breaking down and rebuilding your fires every half hour or so.

STEP 7: TIME AND TEMPERATURE

The target internal temperature for your pork belly is 200°F. It will usually reach this point between 3 to 4 hours into the cook.

Along the way, here is what to expect as it cooks. For the first hour, it will be wet and white on top. As it continues to cook, however, the fat will begin to darken and shrink. The meat will also turn a darker red.

Because of the generous fat cap, you don't need to spritz the meat. Just keep building fires. Each hour, probe the belly in the center, where it's thickest, with the thermometer so you can gauge how far along it is in the cook.

You'll know it's close to being done when the meat has shrunk almost 40 percent, the fat is crisp and golden, and the thermometer slides in like it's going through soft butter. Once it hits 200°F, it's time to pull.

STEP 8: PULL, WRAP, AND REST

When the skin is crispy and bubby with all the fat rendered, and the belly feels tender and plush, it will be time to pull.

We don't wrap our bellies because we want the bark to stay crisp. If we were to wrap them, the bark would soften and not be as texturally interesting.

Instead, we place the bellies on a sheet pan and let them cool to 140°F. At this point, you can either slice and serve them or keep them in a warmer, unwrapped, for several hours before serving.

STEP 9: CUT

Place the belly on the cutting board with the long side facing you.

We begin to slice on the narrow end with our nondominant hand gently resting on top as we work our way down the belly. We don't like the belly too thick, so we cut it into 1/4-inch slices.

Serve with peach glaze on the side for dipping.

STEP 10: QUALITY CONTROL

Pork belly is a very forgiving cut with its generous fat cap and extensive marbling. The goal is to render that top fat so it forms a crisp shell over the meat. You want each bite bursting with juice. The smoke will have added flavor and color to the meat too. It will taste like uncured bacon.

If your belly is too dry, you may have overcooked it. If the belly doesn't have enough smoke, you may want to build more bundle fires. If there isn't enough seasoning or salt, you may want to go a little heavier next cook.

Slicing the pork belly.

PORK BELLY, SHORT VERSION

1 12-pound (5.44-kilogram) boneless, skinless pork belly, or 1 4-pound (1.81-kilogram) boneless, skinless pork belly portion
Coarse black pepper
Seasoned salt (page 200)
Peach glaze (page 194)

Cutting board
10-inch chef's knife
Shakers
Instant-read meat thermometer

Cut the pork belly into three equally sized pieces, lengthwise, if using a full belly. If using a precut pork belly, leave it the size it is. Round off the corners.

To season, start on the meat side and shake on one pass of seasoned salt. Flip over the belly, and give it one pass with pepper and then one pass with seasoned salt on the fatty side.

Place the belly on the smoker, as far from the firebox as possible. Orient the longer side toward the fire.

Build and light a bundle fire with the damper all the way open, and let it burn until it becomes coals. The smoker will probably be at around 250°F.

After the first fire, close the damper halfway and continue to build either bundle fires or log cabin fires, with a goal of getting the smoker to 275°F for the remainder of the cook.

You want to probe the meat in the thick middle every hour to determine its internal temperature and make sure it doesn't overcook. Pull it when it's at 200°F, which typically will occur between hours 3 and 4 of the cook.

Let the meat rest, uncovered, for 1 hour before serving, or place it in a warmer to hold for up to 5 hours.

To slice, begin at the narrower end and work your way down the belly lengthwise, cutting the meat into 1/4-inch slices. Serve warm with peach glaze.

TURKEY BREAST

"Which item on the tray are you going to eat first?" Jonny asked. The barbecue tray was outfitted with most of the menu, including brisket, sausage, ribs, beans, grits, pickles, and bread. There was a small stack of turkey slices on the tray too.

Many pointed toward the brisket, with some heralding our fluffy bread. Others chose ribs or sausage. The responses fell into line with what people typically enjoy and praise about Texas barbecue. What was interesting, though, was that Jonny said he was going straight for the turkey. It's an underrated and underappreciated gem, he explained. And that is the truth.

While turkey is not considered part of the Texas barbecue trinity, which comprises brisket, sausage, and ribs, it has a long-standing role in most Texans' lives. For instance, smoked turkeys are a popular holiday tradition, and on the day before Thanksgiving, you will smell the inviting scent of post oak burning if you drive around rural areas with the windows down.

We also eat turkey year-round in sandwiches, tacos, and soups. Turkey is an accessible and affordable meat that many Texans fully embrace. Why it's been ignored as a part of the Texas barbecue canon is a mystery. We'd like to change that.

Some people believe turkey to be dry, but we work with pre-brined breasts that maintain a juicy texture throughout every bite. Others say that turkey is bland, but its mild foundation allows the seasonings, such as pepper, salt, and smoke, to shine. Last, when we wrap our turkeys, we smother them in creamy butter, which mingles with the juices and makes each slice shine.

Many have said that our turkey is the best they've ever had. We agree—it's so flavorful and moist. Our smoked turkeys are a fine offering, and yours may become your first bite too.

STEP 1: TOOLS

Cutting board
Boning knife
Thermometer
Foil

Our turkey breasts come pre-boned and brined, so there's not much work needed. We use the cutting board and knife to trim off any extraneous fat or cartilage on our turkeys. The foil will be used for wrapping the breasts at the end of the cook.

STEP 2: MEAT

1 5-pound (2.27-kilogram) boneless turkey breast

For simplicity's sake, we cook turkey breasts that have already been trimmed of the bones and fat. When shopping for your turkey breasts, we recommend that you look for the same. Not only does it make for an easier cook, but there's not enough price difference to justify the extra steps, at least for us.

In our experience, most large grocery stores carry boneless turkey breasts, though even our local store, HEB, still leaves on the skin and doesn't brine them. You want the breasts to be full and plump with a healthy pinkish-white color.

STEP 3: TRIMMING

While our restaurant breasts come with both the breastbone and skin already removed, grocery store boneless breasts often still have the skin. You'll want to remove this, as it's thick and won't get crisp and crackly like it would if you were roasting the breast in an oven; instead, the skin will turn rubbery and prevent the meat from receiving as much smoke flavor as it could.

Now, we understand that you might be concerned that removing the only fat from the cut will dry out the meat, but having your meat brined will go far in retaining moisture. With fire management and a thermometer, your breasts will be tender and juicy, and you won't miss the skin at all.

If you do buy a turkey breast with skin, to remove it, first place the breast on the cutting board, skin-side up. With the boning knife, slide it under the skin and cut through the white strands of cartilage that connect the skin to the meat. After making all the cuts and then lifting away the skin, trim any remaining strands.

STEP 4: SEASONING

Coarse black pepper
Seasoned salt (page 200)

If your breast has not been brined, we recommend that you do this first. The brine will ensure a much juicier bird. Our preferred brine is a wet brine that takes only 30 minutes to add moisture and flavor to the meat. The only ingredients are salt, water, and time. However, we recommend playing around by adding different spices and herbs if you like (see box).

We get pre-brined turkeys because we don't have the space to brine them ourselves. Because they're pre-brined, our turkeys are pretty much already seasoned. We might add a light pass of seasoned salt on top, but for a pre-brined turkey, this is mainly for color. For the most part, we hit our breasts with only some black pepper, which gives more flavor and texture.

If your breasts aren't pre-brined and you don't have the time to brine, you will want to be more aggressive with the seasoned salt. We would do two passes of seasoned salt on the back, flip it over, do two passes of black pepper on the top, and then do two more passes of seasoned salt on top of the black pepper.

If, however, you have a brined breast, you need to do only the two passes of black pepper and one pass of seasoned salt on the top.

STEP 5: PLACEMENT ON THE SMOKER

For our turkeys, we shape them up into a more full, round ball before placing them on the smoker. This prevents the thin, pointier end from cooking too quickly and becoming done before the rest of the turkey. We place the turkeys about 4 inches apart on the smoker, with the fuller end pointing toward the fire. We also place the turkeys as far from the fire as possible. We place the turkeys on the smoker immediately after seasoning.

STEP 6: FIRE AND SMOKE

For our first fire, we start with a bundle fire (for more detail, see chapter 5). Turkey cooks quickly, and we want to hit it with as much flavor as possible.

While ultimately we want the smoker to reach 275°F, we start slow. In the first hour, yours may rise only to 250°F, which is fine. You want to be gentle with the heat so the turkey breasts don't get singed. While each smoker is different, for a 90-gallon offset, we'd start with two full logs (or four splits) for the initial burn.

For this first fire, open the damper all the way. Once the fire is lit, close the door almost all the way, leaving it cracked open about an inch. This will pull the smoke through the chamber and allow the wood to burn down and form your bed of coals.

After an hour or so, ideally your smoker will be up to about 250°F. If it's not, don't worry about it too much—it will get there! At this time, the logs will be burnt. With your shovel, break the burnt logs down. Now you have a coal bed.

Build your next fire in a log cabin style or bundle; it's your choice. Lane recommends going with a bundle fire the entire cook if it's the only meat on the smoker. But if you're cooking it with other items that you don't want to get as much smoke, you can do a log cabin style instead.

We also close the damper halfway. This locks in the heat. For the next 3 to 4 hours, you'll be simply breaking down and rebuilding your fires every half hour or so.

Be sure to clean out the ashes from the firebox if there's too much accumulation along the way because you don't want the logs to rise too high. Shoot for a smoker temperature of 275°F during the rest of the cook.

STEP 7: TIME AND TEMPERATURE

The target internal temperature for your turkey is 155°F. It will usually reach this point between 3 to 4 hours into the cook.

Along the way, here is what to expect as it cooks. For the first hour, it will be wet on top. As it continues to cook, however, the meat will begin to dry and transform from white to a darker brown.

Because there's no fat on the turkey, you want to keep an eye on it to make sure that it doesn't overcook. Each hour, probe the breast in the center, where it's thickest, with the thermometer so you can gauge how far along it is in the cook.

Once it hits 155°F, it's time to pull the breast.

STEP 8: PULL, WRAP, AND REST

1 stick unsalted butter per breast

For wrapping the turkey, rip off two 1½-foot-long sheets of foil. We use two sheets to ensure that the butter remains in the packet but also that the delicate meat has a warm cocoon to nestle in as it rests.

When wrapping, we use a lot of butter so that when we unwrap the meat, it's super shiny and moist. To wrap each breast, we first stack the two pieces of foil on top of each other. Place the long sides of the foil facing you.

Place the breast meat-side down in the far left corner. Because the turkey breast is sort of a triangle shape, we take the pointier end and point it toward the corner of the foil. You want the breast to sit about 2 to 3 inches from the edge.

Once you've positioned the breast on the foil, place the cold butter on top of it. Crunch the sides of the foil and then roll the breast twice in it until it's completely wrapped. Tighten the edges of the foil, and the butter will melt down into the sides. When we open up the foil, the butter will have bathed the meat and it will be shiny and pretty.

You can serve the turkey after it's rested for 1 hour, or you can hold it in a warmer for several hours. We don't recommend holding it in a warmer for more than 5 hours, or it will begin to dry and lose its color.

STEP 9: CUT

When you remove the turkey from the foil, flip it onto the cutting board so it lands meat-side up, and then pour the butter and juices from the foil on top of the turkey.

Turkey has a grain, and to cut it, you want to go against this grain so each piece is tender. To position the turkey, place it on the board so that the narrow, pointed end is closest to your cutting hand, with the thicker end closer to your holding hand. The length of the breast will be facing you.

We begin to cut on the narrow end with our non-dominant hand gently resting on top as we work our way down the breast. We cut our breasts into ¼-inch slices, dipping each into the buttery puddle of juices on the board before placing it on the tray.

STEP 10: QUALITY CONTROL

Turkey is pretty chill, so as long as you don't overcook it and it's been properly seasoned either with brine or the seasoned salt, you're mainly looking to see whether it's tender and moist with enough flavor. If you have brined it yourself, for instance, observe whether your post-brine seasoning was enough or too much. Another thing we look at is color—if it's too dark, for instance, you may consider doing only one bundle fire next time, if you did more than one. If there isn't enough color, you may consider more bundle fires or more seasoned salt and/or pepper.

TURKEY BREAST, SHORT VERSION

1 5-pound (2.27-kilogram) boneless turkey breast (preferably brined)
Poultry brine (page 181) (optional)
Seasoned salt (page 200)
Coarse black pepper
1 stick unsalted butter

Cutting board
10-inch chef's knife
Shakers
Instant-read meat thermometer
Foil

Remove any skin or cartilage from the breast. If it hasn't been brined already, prepare the poultry brine, then brine the meat for 30 minutes or up to overnight.

Once the meat has been brined, shake the coarse pepper onto the top side, making 2 passes. Make 1 pass of the seasoned salt.

If you are not using a brined breast, you'll want to season it more. To do this, make 2 passes of the seasoned salt on the bottom of the breast. Flip over the breast, make 2 passes with the coarse pepper, and then make 2 light passes with the seasoned salt.

Place the breast on the smoker, as far from the firebox as possible. Shape the breast into a ball shape, with the thicker end pointing toward the fire.

Build and light a bundle fire with the damper all the way open, and let it burn until it becomes coals. The smoker will probably be at about 250°F.

After the first fire, close the damper halfway and continue to build either bundle fires or log cabin fires to get the smoker to 275°F for the remainder of the cook.

You want to probe the meat in the thick middle every hour to determine its internal temperature and make sure it doesn't overcook. Pull it when it's at 155°F, which typically will occur between hours 3 and 4 of the cook.

Tear off two 1½-foot-long pieces of foil. Stack them on top of each other and then place the breast with the meat side down (grate-side up) in the bottom left corner. Place the butter on top of the meat then crunch the sides over the breast. Roll the foil-wrapped meat in the direction of the diagonally opposite corner twice, then seal all the sides of the foil until tight.

Let the meat rest for 1 hour before serving, or place it in a warmer to hold for up to 5 hours.

When you remove the meat from the foil to serve, shake the butter and juices over the meat and onto the board.

To slice, begin at the more narrow end and work your way down the breast lengthwise, cutting the meat into ¼-inch slices. Dip the slices into the buttery juices. Serve warm.

BRINING YOUR TURKEY

If your turkey breasts are not brined, then we recommend you take the time to add some extra seasoning to the meat before cooking. Even a 30-minute rest in a salt-water bath will add juice and flavor to your breast. Alternatively, you can do a dry brine overnight.

Salt will impart the most flavor, but if you're feeling wild, feel free to throw some herbs or spices into either the wet or dry brine. Garlic, sage, rosemary, citrus zest, and chili powder all go well with the mild flavor of turkey.

WET BRINE

1 gallon warm water
1 cup kosher salt

Fill a food-safe container with the water, then add the salt. Stir until the salt dissolves and then add the breast. Allow it to sit for 30 minutes, refrigerated.

DRY BRINE

½ teaspoon kosher salt per pound of meat

Season the breast all over. Place the breast in a container, covered, then allow it to rest for 1 to 2 days, refrigerated.

SAUSAGE

To cook our sausages after they've been stuffed, we use a process known as a cold smoke. While all other smoker recipes go with temperatures above 250°F, we use a cold smoke temperature of between 150 and 175°F when initially cooking our sausages. This is to hit the meat with the flavor of smoke while still leaving the fat unrendered inside.

If you were to render the fat on the initial cook, then the sausages would be dry. With our cold smoke, however, they gently cook and all the flavors come together, but it's a gentle heat that keeps the structural integrity of the sausage intact.

While this method is for sausage, it's a standard cold smoking technique that could be applied to anything you wish to kiss with smoke without completely cooking the ingredients, such as cheese, sugar, pepper, or even cookie dough.

STEP 1: TOOLS

4-gallon container
Ice
Sheet pan with rack

STEP 2: MEAT

Already stuffed and cased sausage (see chapter 6)

STEP 3: TRIMMING

There is no trimming since the sausages are already stuffed. However, if your strand of sausages has not been cut into individual links yet, we suggest cutting them before smoking.

STEP 4: SEASONING

The sausages are already seasoned, so there is no additional work to be done here.

STEP 5: PLACEMENT ON THE SMOKER

You want to put the rested sausages onto the smoker cold. Don't place them too close to the firebox; otherwise they'll cook too fast and burn a bit. Place them about an inch apart so all sides will color evenly. If any of the sausages are touching, they won't get any color and will have bald spots.

If you don't have time to dry the sausages overnight before cooking, you can place them on the smoker while building the first fire, but leave the chamber doors open. This will dry them out really quickly. After you have your coal bed, you can shut the doors and proceed.

STEP 6: FIRE AND SMOKE

For your first fire, start with a bundle fire so you can build your coal bed. We recommend building your coal bed with the first fire before you place the sausages on the pit.

Once you have your coal bed, on a backyard pit, take a log or two and nestle them into the coal bed. (If you're working on a 1,000-gallon, like we do at the restaurant, you'll want to use three or four logs.)

When surrounded with the coals, they should begin to start smoking quickly. You don't want tall flames; instead, your goal is to have a smoldering, low flame with lots of smoke.

After you've nestled the logs and they've caught fire, close the firebox door all the way. The airflow in a cold smoke comes from the pull of the damper, so open the damper all the way. This keeps the smoke and heat flowing without letting it become too humid in the chamber.

And don't worry about how smoky it is; you can't have clean smoke at 175°F. That smoke is also adding color and flavor!

We cold smoke for about 3 hours. We start at 150°F for the first couple of hours and then go to 175°F for the final hour. Longer cooks don't help the sausage, and the longer you cook it, the more the casing starts to get hard and leathery.

STEP 7: TIME AND TEMPERATURE

About an hour after placing the sausages on the smoker, you'll start to see color on the top side of the sausage. If you touch it, it will also feel dry.

At this time, flip the links over to the other side so this side can get color too. If you want to probe for temperature at this point, it will be about 120°F. You don't want to poke too many holes in your sausages because this will cause them to leak, so we recommend having a tester sausage that takes the brunt of the probing. You'll often have a smaller one at the end of your strand of links, which works great for this. As you cook, keep this in the center of your smoker and probe it for a gauge of how the cook is coming along.

If you want to spritz the sausages, do it at this point. We fill a spritzer with warm water and spritz our sausages. This helps the casing become dry and snappy, almost like paper.

After flipping, continue to cook at 150 to 175°F until the sausages have an internal temperature of 145 to 150°F. If they start to get a bit wrinkly at 140, you may pull them since you'll be cooking them again. But if they're looking smooth, wait until they're between 145 and 150°F, and they'll be perfect. While this will most likely happen in about 3 hours, sometimes it can take up to 5 hours, depending on your pit.

STEP 8: PULL AND REST

Before you pull the sausages, prepare your ice bath. Fill your 4-gallon container with ice and water.

You also want to set up your drying rack. We use a rack that fits into a sheet pan, much like a cookie-cooling rack.

After you pull the sausages, immediately put them into the ice bath. This shock will stop the cook immediately. Leave them in the ice bath for 1 to 2 minutes, then remove the sausages and place them on the prepared rack to dry.

Be sure not to leave them in the ice bath too long

or they'll start to lose color. Two minutes is the most you want to do—they'll be cooled down enough so they don't become overdone.

On the drying rack, you'll want to keep the sausages in one layer, and not stack them. You don't want them touching so they'll dry evenly. But they don't need to be spaced as far apart as they were on the smoker; just give them a bit of breathing room.

If you're curious about what temperature they'll be after the ice bath, it will probably be about 100°F. But we don't recommend probing them with a thermometer to check the temperature, since this will cause juices to leak. Have faith that the ice bath will do its job!

The sausages will shrivel up a bit after sitting in the water, kind of like your fingers do when they get wet. But don't worry about it because when you reheat them to eat, they'll plump up again.

As the sausages dry on the rack, they'll start to regain their color, which is a process we call blooming. We let them rest and bloom until they're dry and at room temperature, which takes about 30 to 40 minutes. Then we refrigerate them uncovered until it's time to reheat them to eat.

To reheat the sausages, we bring them up to room temperature and then cook them at a temperature of 300°F for about 30 minutes or until the sausages have an internal temperature of 145°F. Don't reheat them beyond 150°F or they'll start breaking up and becoming dry.

You can reheat them on a smoker, or you can do it in an oven; either one will work. You will get a better color on the smoker, but the oven does a good job, too, and can be more efficient.

STEP 9: CUT

You can serve the sausages whole, or you can slice them before serving. We cut our sausages into rounds, making ½-inch cuts down the length of the sausage.

STEP 10: QUALITY CONTROL

Because there are so many steps in sausage making and opportunities to test the recipe as you go, hopefully there won't be too many surprises by the time you serve the sausage.

You want your links to have a rich color from the smoke. They will be plump with a taut casing adhering to the meat. If there are any air bubbles, they should be a rare occurrence.

Now take a bite. The ideal casing is tender with a dry, almost crisp texture. The teeth go through it easily. You want the filling to be tender and juicy with a bouncy, smooth texture, not coarse or grainy.

How is the level of salt? How are the spices? If you're eating a jalapeño cheese sausage, are the peppers and cheese well distributed? Does the casing adhere to the meat as you eat, or does it crumble off like burnt paper?

Your first batch of sausage may not be perfect, which is why the quality control stage is so important. For instance, when one apprentice made sausage, everything seemed like it was going well but in the end the texture was terrible, more like a hamburger than a hotdog.

It turned out that she had used brisket trim that had been in the freezer for several months. The lesson learned was to use fresh meat! With that in mind, her next batch was perfect.

If you want to show off your homemade links, you can take a sausage, place your hands on each end, and then snap the sausage in half. Do you hear a snap? When you gently squeeze the sausage, do juices start to escape? If so, you've created a mighty fine link!

THE ART OF THE TRAY

There is no better symbol for the communal spirit of barbecue than the tray, which when arranged with thought, care, and abundance can be its own work of art. Of course, if you're preparing barbecue at home, you may wish to forgo the literal tray, since most likely you will have serving bowls for the side dishes and a platter or carving board for the meats.

When one apprentice would cook the Goldee's menu for friends at home, this was how she offered the meats and accompaniments. What she observed was that the food was so beautiful that it didn't look like restaurant food but dishes that had been prepared with love for a family gathering.

This was the highest compliment one could pay our food, since each week it is indeed like we are feeding a group of loved ones. Even if we haven't met our customers just yet, we love getting to know them as they visit the pit room, sit in the line, and approach the cutting block. We love hearing your stories.

While a communal feast with beautiful bowls and a long table for everyone would be ideal, that's not how our business, or most barbecue businesses, are designed. Hence the tray, which is where the cutter and those portioning out the sides bring every aspect of the meal to one portable place.

There are no right or wrong ways to design a tray, though think about your menu and how the different items balance each other in terms of shape, color, and texture. Also keep in mind the nature of each specific item. For example, brisket may oxidize and not look as gorgeous as when it was first sliced, so you may want to position cubes of burnt ends over the slices, or even layer a few ribs, which keep their color longer, on top.

How do your sides go together in terms of color? For instance, are all your sides white? Think about changing it up by adding red onions, for instance, to a potato salad, or dark green kale to a light green slaw. These are things we've done with our menu, and they were all done with intention. When we designed our menu, we thought about the entire tray working together as one unit.

Look at the composition of everything on the tray. Strive for balance, but also know that odd numbers are more appealing than even. If you have an even number of items, perhaps break it up with the bread and pickles. An odd number of items creates tension and energy, and even if the viewer can't define why it's more appealing, their subconscious is engaged.

One thing to consider if you're a restaurateur is the amount your customers are ordering. For instance, if most are getting two slices of meat and one side, that's going to look empty on a tray. For these smaller orders, a round plate is more visually appealing since the meat and side will fill the plate, once again creating the appearance of abundance.

As for the color of the tray, try not to get one that contrasts with the color of your food menu and the butcher paper you're using. The tray is the frame of your barbecue portrait, and you want it to lead the eye toward the center instead of commanding attention to the food by clashing with the items. We use off-white trays at Goldee's, which are neutral yet stylish. It's also good to have two sizes of trays: big ones for big orders and smaller ones for smaller orders. This way, you'll have more options for making your tray appear bountiful and lush.

8 ALL THE TRIMMIN

GS

While you are waiting in line at Goldee's, you will see a neon sign in the window that reads, "We bake our own bread." At first, you might think it's a joke since bread at a barbecue place is considered nothing more than filler. Most places offer commercial sliced white bread that comes from a plastic bag. It's no surprise that people aren't thrilled with that offering.

At Goldee's, our sign is not a joke but a proclamation. Yes, we smoke all our meats with nothing but wood and time, which takes care and dedication to get everything right. Why wouldn't we apply that same concern and care to everything else on our tray?

When we started creating our menu, we knew that bread would be an equal player and not an afterthought. Who doesn't love a tender, sweet slice of bread cut from a loaf just pulled from the oven? Not only is our bread a great vehicle for sauce or meat, but it's also excellent on its own. Homemade bread was a must.

The rest of our tray followed that philosophy. We wanted to create a menu that celebrated the roots of Central Texas barbecue, but we also wanted to breathe new life into the standard canon. Nothing too crazy, mind you, but our approach was to shower each dish with intention and care from the beginning.

For our salads, we make our dressings from scratch. We also thought about the colors of onions we included and the different textures present in each dish. Our aim for each was to have a visually pleasing and refreshing dish to enhance and complement the rich meats.

We make all of our pickles in-house, and we bake all of our desserts too. These days, we even have a custom recipe for our seasoned salt. Every single bite taken at Goldee's has been pondered and tested multiple times to achieve a level of elegant perfection. We're not trying to reinvent anything; we only want every classic dish to taste as excellent as it can.

When you have such a limited menu, every bite counts. And we give all of our sauces, pickles, sides, and baked goods the same level of care that we give our smoked meats.

WE BAKE
OUR OWN
BREAD

GOLDEE'S BARBECUE SAUCE

We always liked mustard with beef, so it made sense to make a mustard-based barbecue sauce. When we began doing our pop-ups, our initial version was bright yellow. We loved it. But sadly, nobody thought of it as barbecue sauce.

Gradually we added more ketchup, a standard base for Texas barbecue sauce. The color mellowed, but we didn't want ketchup to be the main flavor. Instead, we wanted a balance of the two with neither dominating the sauce.

After many test runs, the version we ended up with and now serve today was loosely inspired by City Market in Luling and the Salt Lick in Driftwood, two Central Texas spots that also have a heavier amount of mustard in their sauces. At the same time, ours has a distinctive flavor that's tangy and sweet. It not only goes well with beef but can be used with poultry and pork, or as a dipping sauce for our bread.

1¾ cups plus 2 tablespoons (469 milliliters) prepared yellow mustard
1¼ cups (313 milliliters) water
1½ cups (375 milliliters) apple cider vinegar
½ cup plus 2 tablespoons (156 milliliters) brown sugar
3½ tablespoons granulated garlic powder
5 teaspoons granulated onion powder
5 teaspoons coarse black pepper
5 teaspoons Worcestershire sauce
1¼ teaspoons chili powder
1¼ teaspoons Korean chili flakes
2 teaspoons kosher salt
½ teaspoon ground cumin
½ teaspoon sweet paprika
2½ cups (625 milliliters) ketchup
2¼ cups (625 milliliters) honey

Place the yellow mustard, water, apple cider vinegar, brown sugar, garlic powder, onion powder, black pepper, Worcestershire sauce, chili powder, Korean chili flakes, salt, cumin, and paprika in a pot, and bring to a boil over high heat.

Remove the pot from the heat, then stir in the ketchup and honey until well blended. Can be stored refrigerated or unrefrigerated for up to 2 weeks.

YIELD: 4 CUPS

RIB GLAZE

Texas Monthly barbecue editor Daniel Vaughn once referred to our rib glaze as a simple syrup of vinegar and sugar. His description is not far from the truth, though we also stir in a handful of spices, Worcestershire, and ketchup to add flavor and depth. We knew we wanted it thin so the ribs wouldn't seem like they were overly sauced. We also wanted it to have lots of sweetness and tanginess so it would make the ribs interesting without being overwhelming.

Dialing in that balance took time. Back when we were living in Austin, every time we taught a class, we'd make a change. It wasn't until we began doing pop-ups before opening at Zavala's in nearby Grand Prairie that we felt confident with it.

It's thinner than a sauce, which is why we call it a glaze. What we're aiming for when we squirt it on our finished racks of pork is color and that final hit of tang and flavor to combine with the meaty ribs and smoke. Sure, it's simple in concept. But each glazed rack will be complex enough to keep eaters reaching for more.

1½ cups (375 milliliters) apple cider vinegar
¾ cup (188 milliliters) ketchup
¼ cup (63 milliliters) water
¼ cup (63 milliliters) Worcestershire sauce
1¼ cups (313 milliliters) white sugar
1 teaspoon kosher salt
½ tablespoon onion powder
½ tablespoon garlic powder
½ tablespoon ground cumin
½ teaspoon ground paprika

Place all ingredients into a pot. Stir until well combined. Bring to a boil over high heat while occasionally stirring, about 5 to 7 minutes.

Remove from the heat. Taste and adjust seasonings if needed. Cover and store. The glaze will keep unrefrigerated for 1 week or refrigerated for 3 weeks.

YIELD: 3 CUPS

PEACH GLAZE

Lane was inspired by the peach glaze found at InterStellar BBQ in Austin, Texas. On the 2021 *Texas Monthly* list, they were ranked number two in the state, right behind us. We're huge fans of their smoked meats and culinary creativity, and when we were trying to find a tangy and sweet sauce to go with our smoked pork belly, we followed their path and combined peaches with juice and sugar.

At the restaurant, we work with a simple peach jam. One of our recipe testers, however, made this with jalapeño-peach jam, and if you're so inclined, she declared it a fine adaptation.

2½ cups (625 milliliters) peach jam
⅓ cup (83 milliliters) white vinegar
¼ cup (63 milliliters) orange juice
2 tablespoons lemon juice
½ cup (125 milliliters) granulated sugar
1 teaspoon kosher salt
½ tablespoon garlic powder
½ tablespoon onion powder
1 teaspoon mustard powder
½ teaspoon white pepper
¼ teaspoon cayenne powder

In a saucepan, whisk together all ingredients until well blended. Place on the stove and cook on medium-low heat until slightly reduced and thickened, about 15 to 20 minutes.

Taste and make any adjustments you desire. Serve with smoked pork belly or as a rib glaze.

YIELD: ABOUT 2½ CUPS

OLD SCHOOL BRISKET SAUCE

This was our chopped beef sandwich sauce when we first opened Goldee's. It's an adaptation of the recipe served at Louis Mueller Barbecue in Taylor, Texas, which is said to have been developed by pitmaster Fred Fountaine when he started running the Mueller pits in 1946.

It harkens back to older Texas barbecue sauces that combine ketchup, onions, butter, chili powder, and vinegar. It takes time to make, but the slow cook yields a savory sauce that feels both fresh and nostalgic with its classic Texas taste.

½ stick (56 grams) unsalted butter
1 whole white onion, sliced
½ tablespoon kosher salt
1 tablespoon sweet paprika
2 teaspoons black pepper
3 teaspoons chili powder
1 teaspoon ground cumin
⅓ teaspoon garlic powder
2 tablespoons brown sugar
3 cups (750 milliliters) pork stock or water
1 8-ounce (225-gram) can of tomato sauce
2 tablespoons apple cider vinegar
2 tablespoons Worcestershire sauce
1 teaspoon jalapeño hot sauce (page 196)

In a medium pot, melt the butter on medium-low heat. Add the onions and cook until softened, stirring occasionally, about 15 minutes.

Stir in the salt and cook for 1 minute. Add to the pot the paprika, black pepper, chili powder, ground cumin, and garlic powder, and cook for 1 minute.

Stir into the pot the brown sugar, pork stock, tomato sauce, apple cider vinegar, Worcestershire sauce, and hot sauce.

Turn the heat to high and boil uncovered for 20 minutes. Turn the heat to low, then simmer uncovered for 40 minutes or until the sauce is reduced and the onions are super tender. Taste and adjust seasonings if desired.

YIELD: ABOUT 1 QUART

JALAPEÑO HOT SAUCE

We used to go to Kreuz Market in Lockhart often, and when we ordered their sausage, we'd put it on a cracker with their hot sauce. It was really good. We loved its simplicity and bite, and wanted to have this at our spot too. Our hot sauce also tastes good with our cheese grits and beans, or even drizzled onto our meats.

1 pound (454 grams) whole jalapeños, seeded and stemmed
2 tablespoons kosher salt
1½ cups (375 milliliters) white vinegar
½ teaspoon xanthan gum

Place the jalapeños and salt in a blender or food processor, then process until finely ground.

Place the ground jalapeños into a quart-size jar, cover the jar, and let rest for 24 hours.

Stir in the vinegar, then allow it to ferment, covered, for 1 week in a dark place.

After a week has passed, the peppers and vinegar should be a dark army green. Strain the hot sauce through a colander, then stir the xanthan gum into the liquid to stabilize.

Refrigerate. The sauce will keep for 1 month.

YIELD: 1½ CUPS

Note: You can find xanthan gum at specialty grocery stores, vitamin/nutrition stores, Target, Walmart, or online.

JEOW SOM

This piquant Laotian dipping sauce gets its brightness from lime juice and its heat from Thai chili peppers. There's also an underlying savory funk from the fish sauce, which keeps you coming back for more. We serve it with Lao Texas sausage, though it also pairs well with our pork belly.

¼ cup (63 milliliters) freshly squeezed lime juice
2 tablespoons fish sauce
3 cloves garlic, chopped
2 fresh Thai chilies, stemmed, seeded, and chopped
2 tablespoons granulated sugar
½ teaspoon kosher salt
1 tablespoon chopped cilantro

Place the lime juice, fish sauce, garlic, chilies, sugar, and salt in a blender or food processor, and blend until well combined.

Stir in the cilantro, then taste. Make any adjustments you desire.

YIELD: 1 CUP

LIME CREMA

We top our Texas chili (page 216) with a generous scoop of crema. It's a Mexican cultured cream that is thick and tangy, much like sour cream. Sure, you could purchase either Mexican crema or sour cream. But once you learn how simple it is to prepare at home, you'll wonder why you hadn't been making it before.

2 cups (500 milliliters) heavy whipping cream
¼ cup (63 milliliters) buttermilk
2 whole garlic cloves, minced
2 tablespoons freshly squeezed lime juice
1 tablespoon fresh lime zest
1⅛ teaspoons kosher salt

Stir together the heavy whipping cream and buttermilk in a jar, then cover and let it ferment at room temperature for 48 hours.

After it's fermented and thickened, stir in the garlic, lime juice, lime zest, and salt. Cover and refrigerate. Stir before using. The crema will keep refrigerated for 1 week.

YIELD: 2¼ CUPS

GOLDEE'S HOUSE PICKLES

We started preparing our cucumber house pickles back in Austin when we wanted an accompaniment that wasn't too sour but still tart enough to break up the richness of the meat. When we first began making the pickles, we'd do a week-long brine, but these days we no longer have the space for that. That's okay—we've come up with a method that takes only an hour, and we feel that they're just as tasty and crisp.

1½ pounds (680 grams) pickling cucumbers, cut into thin coins
2 ounces (57 grams) fresh dill
4 cloves garlic, smashed
2 cups (500 milliliters) water
2 cups (500 milliliters) white vinegar
¼ cup (63 milliliters) sugar
2 tablespoons kosher salt
2 teaspoons mustard seed
2 teaspoons black peppercorns
2 teaspoons coriander seeds
1½ teaspoons dill seed
1 bay leaf

Place the cucumbers, dill, and garlic into a 2-quart container.

Place the water, white vinegar, sugar, salt, mustard seed, peppercorns, coriander seeds, dill seed, and bay leaf in a medium pot, and bring to a boil over high heat. When the mixture is boiling, pour over the cucumbers.

Cover and refrigerate for at least 1 hour, then serve. The pickles will keep for 1 week.

YIELD: 2 QUARTS

PICKLED JALAPEÑOS AND CARROTS

After Cecilia joined our restaurant team, she shared with us her family's recipe for pickled jalapeños and carrots. While we had sometimes made pickled jalapeños with our traditional sweet pickle brine, her version was livelier and more tangy, and we gladly let her take over the jalapeño pickle shift.

Her recipe uses whole jalapeño chilies, though you could slice them into rounds if you prefer. She also adds Mexican oregano, red chili flakes, and carrots, which not only add an herbal hint but also give each serving a beautiful hit of orange color. On Thursdays, when she makes her weekly batch, the kitchen is filled with the zesty aroma of peppers and aromatics. If you love jalapeños, it smells like heaven.

2 pounds (907 grams) whole jalapeños
1 pound (454 grams) whole carrots
3 cups (750 milliliters) white vinegar
3 cups (750 milliliters) water
2 tablespoons kosher salt
½ tablespoon Mexican oregano
½ tablespoon red chili flakes
1 teaspoon mustard seeds
1 teaspoon black peppercorns
1 teaspoon coriander seeds
¼ white onion, sliced

With a sharp knife, cut an X-shape into the top end of each jalapeño.

Slice the carrots into ¼-inch rounds.

In a large pot, combine the vinegar, water, salt, oregano, red chili flakes, mustard seeds, peppercorns, and coriander seeds, and bring to a boil.

Once the water and vinegar mixture is boiling, add the jalapeños. Blanch in the boiling liquid for about 4 minutes or until all the jalapeños shift from a bright green to a more muted green.

Once the jalapeños are done, remove them from the boiling brine with a slotted spoon and place them in a wide-mouth 2-quart jar or food-safe container.

Add the carrots to the boiling brine and blanch for 4 minutes. Once done, turn off the heat, remove the carrots with a slotted spoon, and place them on top of the jalapeños.

Lay the onions on top of the carrots, then pour the hot brine over everything.

Let cool to room temperature and refrigerate overnight.

YIELD: 2 QUARTS

GOLDEE'S SEASONED SALT

For years, the barbecue world's biggest secret was that pitmasters were using Lawry's seasoning salt to the traditional combination of black pepper and salt. We were no strangers to this practice, and from the beginning we've used seasoned salt on all our meats.

While Lawry's will always be our first love, we wanted to branch out and create our own signature blend. Lane began with table salt, turmeric, and garlic, which are the foundation of Lawry's. Paprika also plays a role in Lawry's. However, we found that this bright-red spice adds color but little flavor, so we swapped in chili powder for that. Lane also loves the acidity that comes with white pepper, which adds some zest to the savory notes. Celery salt and a bit of sugar balance out the blend.

5 tablespoons table salt
1 tablespoon crushed beef bouillon
2 teaspoons brown sugar
1 tablespoon chili powder
½ teaspoon ground turmeric
1½ teaspoons garlic salt
1½ teaspoons celery salt
½ teaspoon white pepper
½ teaspoon cornstarch
¼ teaspoon cayenne powder

Stir all ingredients together. Taste and make adjustments if desired. Seasoned salt will keep in an airtight container for 3 months.

YIELD: ABOUT ⅔ CUP

TALLOW

When we trim our briskets, we're left with lots of soft fat. It's not great for sausage, so we render it and make tallow instead. Primarily, we use it when wrapping our briskets to keep them shiny and moist.

However, it's also a delicious cooking fat in dishes such as our collard greens (page 213) and Texas chili (page 216). It gives homemade biscuits (page 222) a savory, flaky appeal. And one time we ran out of butter at the restaurant, so we substituted softened tallow in our bread dough instead. Not one customer complained.

2 pounds (907 grams) soft brisket fat, cubed
Water

Preheat the oven to 250°F.

Put the fat in a large pot. Add water to cover, then place the pot in the oven and cook uncovered for 4 hours or until the fat is rendered and liquid.

Strain the tallow, then chill. It will keep refrigerated in an air-tight container for 1 month.

YIELD: 2 QUARTS

PORK STOCK

After we've trimmed countless racks of ribs, we're left with a pile of bones. We make a simple pork stock with our bounty, which we then use in our side dishes, such as beans. This is a purist stock of only meat and bones with no aromatics, salt, or seasonings. Feel free to enhance it as you wish.

1 pound (454 grams) pork rib bones with meat
10 cups (2.5 liters) water

Cover the bones with water. Bring to a boil and simmer for 4 hours. Strain and store refrigerated for up to 1 week.

YIELD: 2 QUARTS

GOLDEE'S CHEESE GRITS

Jonny doesn't like macaroni and cheese at barbecue restaurants because it's hard to keep fresh while it sits on the steam table during service, and the result is it's often coagulated and inconsistent. But we still wanted a creamy side dish, so Lane suggested cheese grits. He'd seen them served at barbecue spots, and he knew that if we came up with our own version, customers would be satisfied. Plus, we can give them a quick stir during service, and their texture will remain rich and smooth.

We use quick yellow grits, which have more texture and flavor than instant grits but don't take nearly as long to cook as slow grits. The grits we buy are made by Bob's Red Mill. They get their flavor and color from salt, coarse red pepper, and crushed Korean red chili. We use both cream cheese and sharp yellow cheddar, the former giving the dish a lush texture and the latter adding color and a cheesy tang. To finish, we splash in apple cider vinegar or our jalapeño hot sauce, which brightens up this rich dish and invites you to eat more.

4 cups (1 liter) water
1 cup (250 milliliters) whole milk
1 tablespoon kosher salt
½ teaspoon crushed Korean red chili
¼ teaspoon coarse black pepper
1 cup (250 milliliters) quick (not instant) yellow grits
4 tablespoons unsalted butter
2 ounces (57 grams) cream cheese
4 ounces (113 grams) sharp yellow cheddar, shredded
1 tablespoon apple cider vinegar or jalapeño hot sauce (page 196)

Place the water, milk, salt, red chili, and black pepper in a pot, then bring to a boil over high heat.

Add the grits, reduce the heat to medium-low, and cook until thickened, stirring frequently, about 5 to 7 minutes.

Add the butter and cream cheese, and stir until melted, about 5 minutes. (You may need to smash some of the cream cheese with your spoon along the side of the pot if it's stubborn and won't melt all the way.)

Stir in the cheese and vinegar, remove from the heat, and cover the pot until the cheese has melted.

YIELD: 8 SERVINGS

GOLDEE'S COLESLAW

When we started testing recipes for the coleslaw, we wanted a balanced version that had both sweet and tangy notes in order to appeal to many people. We began with a more straightforward version that used a buttermilk dressing. It was creamy, but we found it kind of bland and felt it tasted like everybody else's.

One day, Dylan and Lane were playing around with Dijon mustard and lemon juice, and they liked the vinaigrette the two ingredients formed with apple cider vinegar. After that, we decided to toss it with shredded green cabbage along with slivers of red onion and mint for color.

The red onion stayed, but the mint turned black and the slaw wouldn't hold long enough for service. Enter handfuls of curly dark green kale, which added the color and texture contrasts we craved. The result is a refreshing foil to the rich meat that clears the palate. Even those who don't usually enjoy coleslaw tell us that this is the best they've ever had. We agree.

FOR THE DRESSING

1 clove garlic, minced
3 tablespoons Dijon mustard
¼ cup (63 milliliters) white sugar
¼ cup (63 milliliters) apple cider vinegar
2 tablespoons freshly squeezed lemon juice
1 tablespoon fresh lemon zest
1 teaspoon kosher salt
¾ cup (188 milliliters) safflower oil

FOR THE SLAW

8 cups (2 liters) shredded green cabbage
½ red onion, thinly sliced
4 cups (1 liter) chopped curly-leaf kale
1 tablespoon kosher salt
½ tablespoon black pepper

To make the dressing, stir together the garlic, mustard, sugar, vinegar, lemon juice, lemon zest, and salt until well combined. Pour in the oil, and whisk until well blended and emulsified. Taste and make adjustments if desired.

To make the slaw, in a large mixing bowl stir together the cabbage, red onion, kale, salt, pepper, and dressing. Chill for 1 hour, then serve.

YIELD: 8 SERVINGS

GOLDEE'S PINTO BEANS

To our first pop-up in Austin, Nupohn's mother brought baked beans. We enjoyed the dish, but for our future restaurant, we decided we preferred our beans more savory. Using the baked bean recipe as a springboard, we took guidance from Lane's boss, who was obsessed with Gebhardt's chili powder. Adding generous scoops of that into our batch, as well as getting rid of the traditional baked bean ingredients such as ketchup and mustard, we ended up with a bean dish that has a hint of sweetness but also kick and earthiness from the spices and chilies. Stirring in chopped smoked brisket gives it that final layer of barbecue flavor.

1 pound (454 grams) pinto beans
1½ tablespoons kosher salt
2 tablespoons tallow (page 201) or soybean oil
1 whole white onion, cut into slivers
2 fresh jalapeños, seeded, stemmed, and cut into strips
4 fresh garlic cloves, minced
2 tablespoons chili powder, preferably Gebhardt's
½ tablespoon white sugar
1 teaspoon granulated onion
1 teaspoon granulated garlic
1 teaspoon coarse black pepper
1 teaspoon ground cumin
1 bay leaf
4 cups (1 liter) pork stock (page 201) or chicken broth
2 cups (500 milliliters) water
¼ pound (113 grams) chopped smoked brisket
1 10-ounce (283-gram) can tomatoes with green chilies and their juices
½ tablespoon jalapeño hot sauce (196)

Place the beans in a large pot. Add 2 quarts of cold water and the salt, then allow the beans to soak uncovered overnight.

Drain and rinse the beans in a colander after soaking.

In the same pot you used to soak the beans, heat the tallow over medium-low heat. Add the onion and jalapeños, and cook until they are softened and beginning to brown, stirring occasionally, about 5 minutes.

Stir in the garlic and cook for 1 minute. Stir in the chili powder, sugar, granulated onion, granulated garlic, black pepper, cumin, and bay leaf, and cook for 1 minute.

Return the beans to the pot. Add the stock and water. Bring the pot to a boil, partially cover, turn the heat down to low, and simmer for 2 to 3 hours or until tender.

When the beans are tender, stir in the brisket, tomatoes, and jalapeño hot sauce. Cook uncovered for 15 minutes, then taste and adjust seasonings if desired.

YIELD: 8 SERVINGS

Note: If your brisket is particularly fatty, the beans may be greasy on top. You can smash some with a wooden spoon along the side of the pot to help absorb some of the grease. Don't skim the grease, though, as it adds flavor!

GOLDEE'S POTATO SALAD

We were going for a Texas vibe with our potato salad. In Texas, potato salad is traditionally mustard based, but for our dressing, we combine our homemade mayonnaise with prepared yellow mustard. We also dial up the freshness with an abundance of red onion, parsley, pickles, and green onions.

This blend makes the salad creamy and tangy. It also makes our salad appealing to most people. If you've never made homemade dressing before, don't worry—it comes together easily in the blender. After the dressing chills, you'll want to whisk it again before pouring, as it may separate.

FOR THE DRESSING

1 large egg
¼ teaspoon sweet paprika
2 tablespoons white sugar
6 tablespoons apple cider vinegar
2 tablespoons prepared yellow mustard
1 cup (250 milliliters) safflower oil
½ teaspoon kosher salt
½ teaspoon coarse black pepper

FOR THE SALAD

3 pounds (1.36 kilograms) unpeeled Yukon gold potatoes, whole
1 tablespoon kosher salt
3 celery ribs, diced
¾ cup (188 milliliters) diced red onion
4 stalks green onion, green part only, sliced
¼ cup (63 milliliters) chopped Italian parsley
¼ cup (63 milliliters) diced Goldee's house pickles (page 198) or dill pickles

To make the dressing, place the egg, paprika, sugar, vinegar, mustard, oil, salt, and pepper into a blender or food processor, and blend until thick and creamy. Chill until ready to use.

Place the potatoes in a large pot. Cover with cold water, then bring to a boil over high heat. Turn the heat down to medium and cook until fork tender, about 15 to 20 minutes.

Drain the potatoes, then place them in a mixing bowl and toss with the salt. Allow them to cool to room temperature, then mash lightly, leaving bite-size pieces.

Stir the celery, red onion, green onion, parsley, and pickles into the mashed potatoes. Also stir in your prepared dressing until well blended with the potatoes.

Taste and adjust seasonings as desired. Chill for at least 1 hour before serving. The salad and dressing will keep for 3 days in the refrigerator.

YIELD: 2 QUARTS

STICKY RICE

Our co-owner Nupohn and his brother PJ, who also works at Goldee's, are Laotian, and they will quickly tell you that every Laotian meal comes with a side of sticky rice. This glutinous rice yields plump grains that do indeed stick together. When serving Lao Texas sausage, we recommend also offering sticky rice on the side.

1 cup (250 milliliters) long-grain sticky rice

SPECIAL EQUIPMENT

Sticky rice basket or mesh colander
Cheesecloth or tea towel

Place the sticky rice in a bowl and add water to cover, with 3 inches on top. Cover and let soak at room temperature for at least 2 hours but preferably overnight. This is because the longer it soaks, the softer it will be. After it's soaked, strain the rice, then rinse.

Line a steamer basket or mesh colander with cheesecloth. Spoon the drained rice into the prepared steamer basket or colander, and pat the rice so it's even on top.

Place the steamer basket or colander into a pot large enough to contain it. Add enough water to the pot to reach just under the bottom of the steamer (you don't want the water to touch the rice).

Bring the pot to a boil over high heat. Cover the pot, then turn the heat down to low and steam for 40 to 45 minutes or until the rice is tender and translucent.

Once the rice is tender, turn off the heat. Fluff the rice with a wooden spoon, then either serve immediately or leave the rice covered in the steamer until ready to serve.

The rice is best eaten within a couple of hours because it does not stay fresh very long. At Goldee's and in Laos, we portion out individual servings and wrap them in plastic before serving. Sticky rice can hold for a couple of days unrefrigerated and about 4 days refrigerated.

YIELD: 3 CUPS RICE

Notes: When dealing with cooked sticky rice, it is important to store the rice in something that doesn't allow air to touch it. If the rice gets exposed to air, it will dry out and get cold. If you have leftovers, you can wrap them tightly in plastic wrap. Once the rice has a yellowish tint to it, however, it's time to toss it out.

KENNEDALE PORK HASH

Pork hash is a side dish that's a good way to use the leftovers from whole-hog cooking. It's a blend of slowly stewed pork that's served over rice, much like a gravy.

Even though the dish's provenance is in South Carolina, we first encountered it in Austin at the restaurants LeRoy and Lewis and Banger's. Both spots follow the traditional method of using the leftovers from a smoked whole hog. But since we don't cook this meat, we instead use trimmings from our pork ribs.

Ours also veers from the standard since we boil the meat. So, it's not smoky but simply meaty. Its heavy hits of yellow mustard, vinegar, and Worcestershire sauce also give it a sharp and engaging flavor, which goes well with rice. Sure, it may not be the prettiest dish, but it tastes fantastic. Take that first bite, and we know you'll soon be dipping into our gravy and rice for another.

FOR THE PORK

2 pounds (907 grams) pork rib trim or pork shoulder, cubed
2½ cups (625 milliliters) pork stock (page 201) or chicken stock
1 whole yellow onion, roughly chopped
3 whole garlic cloves
1 tablespoon kosher salt

FOR THE FINISHING SAUCE

1 tablespoon coarse black pepper
1 tablespoon garlic powder
1 tablespoon onion powder
1 tablespoon paprika
¾ cup (188 milliliters) prepared yellow mustard
3 tablespoons white vinegar
1½ tablespoons packed brown sugar
1½ teaspoons jalapeño hot sauce (page 196)
1½ teaspoons Worcestershire sauce

Cooked rice, for serving
Green onions, chopped, green part only, for garnishing

Place the pork, pork stock, onion, garlic, and salt into a large pot.

Bring the pot to a boil over high heat, then turn the heat down to low and simmer for 1½ hours or until the pork is tender.

Once the pork is tender, for the finishing sauce, stir in the pepper, garlic powder, onion powder, paprika, mustard, vinegar, brown sugar, hot sauce, and Worcestershire sauce. Cook for 15 minutes.

Blend with an immersion blender or, once cooled, in a regular blender. Taste and adjust seasonings, then serve warm over cooked rice, garnished with green onions.

YIELD: 8 SERVINGS

Note: Instead of making the finishing sauce, you can save time by substituting 1 cup of Goldee's barbecue sauce (page 192).

COLLARD GREENS WITH SMOKED PORK RIBS

When we first opened, we had collard greens on our menu. While we no longer offer them because of space and time considerations, there are customers from our early days who still ask when they're going to return. Our inspiration for these came from Lane's family, who make an excellent pot of greens.

While our version is based on a traditional blend of slowly simmered collards with aromatics, we made them into our own thing by throwing slices of leftover smoked ribs into the pot. The blend of smoke, spice, and pepper elevate these collards into perhaps the best you've ever tried. One bite, and you'll understand why people request that we bring them back.

1 pound (454 grams) collard greens
1 tablespoon tallow (page 201)
1 whole white onion, cut into slivers
2 whole cloves garlic, sliced
1¼ teaspoons kosher salt
½ teaspoon white sugar
¼ teaspoon coarse black pepper
½ teaspoon crushed red pepper flakes
1 cup (250 milliliters) pork stock (page 201)
2 smoked pork ribs (page 157)
4 teaspoons apple cider vinegar

After washing the collard greens, cut out the stems and ribs. Stack the greens, then roll them lengthwise. Cut slices from the entire roll at 1-inch intervals. You should now have lots of collard green strips.

In a large pot, melt the tallow over medium-low heat. Add the onion slivers and cook, stirring occasionally, until they are beginning to brown, about 5 minutes. Stir in the garlic and cook for 1 minute.

Stir in the salt, sugar, pepper, and red pepper flakes, and cook for 1 minute. Add the collard green strips and stock to the pot, turn the heat to high, and bring to a boil. Then turn the heat down to low, cover, and cook the collard greens until they're tender, about 45 minutes.

Remove the rib meat from the bones and then cut the meat into ½-inch cubes. Discard the bones or use them for pork stock.

Once the collard greens are tender, stir in the rib meat and vinegar, and cook for 15 more minutes. Taste and adjust seasonings.

Serve warm.

YIELD: 8 SERVINGS

CHOPPED BEEF SANDWICH

Chopped beef is how we serve the portion of our briskets that can't be offered as clean slices. While the meat is plenty juicy and smoky, its loose structure makes it more stringy than tight and neat. What's fun about chopped beef is the freedom to toss the meat with any sauce, or even just leave it plain. The key is to find a good balance.

At Goldee's, we add our Goldee's barbecue sauce (page 192) to our chopped beef. When we developed this mustard-based condiment, we had beef in mind, and the sauce's blend of tang and sweetness is an excellent foil to the rich meat's texture and flavor.

In our early days, however, we wanted to emulate one of our favorite old school restaurants, Louie Mueller Barbecue in Taylor. They offer a warm sauce that's heavy on ketchup and onions, so we created our old school brisket sauce (page 195) as an homage. It's different from our barbecue sauce but still yields a beefy, saucy bite.

1 pound (454 grams) smoked fatty brisket
¼ cup (63 milliliters) Goldee's barbecue sauce (page 192) or old school brisket sauce (page 195)
4 buns, for serving
Goldee's house pickles (page 198), for serving
Sliced onions, for serving

Gather the fatty pieces of smoked brisket, such as from the mohawk, that won't slice evenly. Either pull the meat into strands with your hands or chop with a knife until a tangle of beef is formed.

Blend the chopped brisket with the sauce. Serve on buns with pickles and onions.

YIELD: 4 CHOPPED BEEF SANDWICHES

TEXAS CHILI

During the pandemic, we were craving a bowl of chili, which is the state dish of Texas. (The state dish is not brisket, but that's another topic for another day.) Lane created a batch that was nothing too crazy, as he says. Instead, it's a take on a classic Texas chili, which means it's prepared with only meat, chili peppers, and spices—the traditional ingredients. And yes, there are no beans, as is also standard.

When Lane lived in Austin, he became passionate about chili peppers. This carried over into his creation of this recipe, and Lane chose to go with the less traditional guajillo chili because he likes its fruity, earthy flavor. It's good on its own in a bowl, though it works well in a Frito pie too. For the meat, we use brisket trimmings. They take more time to become tender, but their rich flavor is a fine vehicle for the earthy, bittersweet chili gravy.

2 ounces (57 grams) (10 to 12, depending on size) dried guajillo chilies, seeded and stemmed
5 cups (1.25 liters) pork stock (page 201) or water
¼ cup (63 milliliters) tallow (page 201)
2 pounds (907 grams) brisket trim (preferably from the mohawk), cut into ½-inch (1¼-centimeter) cubes (rough grind)
2 teaspoons kosher salt
2 teaspoons coarse black pepper
1 small yellow onion, chopped
6 cloves garlic, minced
2 whole jalapeños, stemmed, seeded, and diced
2 tablespoons ground cumin
1 tablespoon garlic powder
1 tablespoon onion powder
½ tablespoon ground coriander
2 whole bay leaves
2 tablespoons masa harina
1 tablespoon white sugar (optional)
1½ tablespoons jalapeño hot sauce (page 196)

In a dry skillet heated over high heat, toast the guajillo chilies for about 10 seconds, turning once. Pour the pork stock into the skillet. Leave the heat on until the stock begins to boil, then turn off the heat and let the chilies soak until soft, about 30 minutes.

Once the chilies are softened, pour the chilies and pork stock into a blender and puree until smooth.

In a large pot, melt the tallow over medium-low heat. Season the brisket on all sides with half the salt and pepper, then add to the pot. While stirring occasionally, cook until browned, about 10 minutes. You may have to do this in batches.

With a slotted spatula, remove the meat from the pot and place it into a large bowl.

Still cooking on medium-low, add the remaining

tallow to the pot. Then, after it's melted, add the onions and jalapeños. Stir and cook until the onions and jalapeños are softened, about 5 minutes. Stir in the garlic, and cook for 1 minute or until it becomes fragrant. Stir in the cumin, garlic powder, onion powder, ground coriander, bay leaves, and the remaining salt and pepper, and cook for 1 minute.

Return the brisket and any accumulated juices to the pot. Pour the guajillo puree into the pot. Bring the pot to a boil over high heat, then reduce the heat to low and cook, partially covered, for 2 to 3 hours or until the brisket is tender, stirring occasionally. Add more liquid if the chili level gets too low.

Once the brisket is tender, stir in the masa harina, sugar, and jalapeño hot sauce, then taste and adjust the seasonings if desired. Simmer uncovered for 15 more minutes.

YIELD: 4 CUPS

GOLDEE'S WHITE BREAD

We always knew that we wanted to serve homemade bread in our restaurant. Jalen will tell you that making bread is one of the most chill jobs at the restaurant, which is good news since making the 130 loaves every week for service is everyone's responsibility.

In most barbecue spots, the bread on the tray comes from a white commercial loaf produced by companies such as Wonder or Mrs. Baird's. There's nothing wrong with using this bread, as its squishy nature makes a fine wrap for sausage. It also works well as a means to scoop up pickles, sauce, and meat.

Our dough, which is close to a standard egg-based brioche loaf, is cold fermented in the refrigerator. This allows the dough to develop more flavor as it slowly rises over a couple of days. We also add a bit more sugar. Our method of adding the fat and sugar last when preparing the dough helps to develop more gluten, which creates a sturdier product.

5½ cups (1.38 liters) bread flour
¾ cup plus 2 tablespoons (219 milliliters) whole milk, room temperature
¾ cup plus 2 tablespoons (219 milliliters) water, room temperature
2 large eggs
1½ teaspoons instant dry yeast
10 tablespoons unsalted butter, room temperature
⅔ cup (167 milliliters) white sugar
1 tablespoon kosher salt

Place a dough hook on a stand mixer. Add the bread flour, milk, water, egg, and yeast to the mixer's bowl, then mix on low until a ball forms, about 3 to 5 minutes.

Cut the butter into four pieces and add them to the mixer. Mix until the butter is fully incorporated into the dough, about 5 minutes.

Add the sugar and salt to the mixing bowl, then continue to mix until the dough is wrapped around the dough hook, about 10 minutes.

Lightly grease a separate mixing bowl with either butter or nonstick cooking spray, then place the dough into the bowl. Cover, then let it rise at room temperature for 1 hour or until the dough doubles in size.

Lightly grease a 9-by-5-inch bread pan, and place the dough into the pan. Cover the pan, then refrigerate for between 12 and 36 hours.

When you're ready to bake the bread, remove the pan from the refrigerator. Allow it to come up to room temperature and rise to the top of the pan while covered, about 2 to 3 hours.

Heat the oven to 370°F. Bake for 20 to 25 minutes or until the bread is light brown on top with a hollow-sounding bottom, and/or it has an internal temperature of 190°F in the center of the loaf.

YIELD: 1 LOAF

Notes: At the restaurant, we use the Ikea Vardargen loaf pan, which is 1.9 quarts in volume. If you have this pan, you may prefer to use it instead of the more standard 9-by-5. The recipe will work in both sizes, however, so a special trip to Ikea isn't necessary.

TALLOW BISCUITS

If you're taking your new smoker for a test drive, the biscuit test (page 69) is a fine way to ascertain all of your hot spots. But you certainly don't need a smoker to whip up a batch of these biscuits, which are tender and flaky from beef tallow.

2 cups (250 milliliters) all-purpose flour
1 tablespoon baking powder
2 tablespoons white sugar
½ teaspoon kosher salt
¼ cup (63 milliliters) tallow, chilled (page 201)
¼ cup (63 milliliters) unsalted butter, chilled
¾ cup (188 milliliters) half-and-half

Preheat the oven to 450°F, and grease a baking sheet or a large ovenproof skillet.

Whisk together the flour, baking powder, sugar, and salt.

Cube the tallow and butter, then work the tallow and butter into the flour mixture with your hands or a pastry blender until the flour is crumbly.

Stir in the half-and-half, mixing until the dough is well combined. It's okay if the dough is a little sticky.

Pour the dough onto a floured surface and knead for 1 minute. The dough should be smooth and no longer wet. (You can sprinkle more flour on the surface if you find that it's sticking.)

Roll out the dough to a ¼-inch thickness, then fold in half. Form the dough into a rectangle, then cut the dough with a knife into eight equal squares.

Alternatively, you can use a round cutter to cut the biscuits from the folded dough. (If you go with round biscuits, you may have to gather the scraps and roll out again if you run out of room while cutting.)

Place the cut biscuits close together on the greased baking sheet (so they will rise up, not out). Bake on the middle rack for 15 minutes or until the tops are golden brown.

YIELD: 8 BISCUITS

GOLDEE'S BANANA PUDDING

When coming up with desserts, we tested banana pudding recipes for a month straight. But they never tasted right. It took us a while, but we finally figured out that bananas were the problem.

Don't get us wrong—we're not anti-banana. We prefer the flavor of super-ripe bananas, but they're a pain to deal with when you're holding pudding for any length of time. They turn too dark and are slimy to cut.

Eventually, we decided that it was much easier to just eliminate them. Yes, the secret ingredient in our banana pudding is no bananas. But no one seems to mind. We make a rich and creamy custard out of egg yolks, milk, butter, and vanilla. To finish, we layer it with a crumble made with crushed vanilla wafers that have been doctored with butter, salt, and cinnamon.

The combination of the rich custard with the pebbly crumble is unique, and not one customer has ever complained about the lack of bananas. In fact, many have said it is the best banana pudding they've ever had.

2 cups (500 milliliters) whole milk
½ cup (125 milliliters) white sugar
¼ teaspoon kosher salt
5 large egg yolks, room temperature
¼ cup (63 milliliters) cornstarch
2 tablespoons unsalted butter
2 teaspoons vanilla extract
1 batch Goldee's banana pudding crumble (page 224)

Add the milk, sugar, and salt to a pot, and heat over medium-low heat until the sugar is dissolved and the milk is warm, about 3 minutes. Remove from the heat.

Beat together the egg yolks and the cornstarch. When the milk is warm, take 2 tablespoons from the pot and stir it into the yolk mixture so you can temper the eggs.

Pour the yolks into the pot with the milk, then return to the heat. Turn the heat up to medium, and while stirring, cook until the mixture is thickened, about 3 minutes.

Remove the pan from the heat, then stir in the butter and vanilla. Once the butter has melted, cover and cool.

Refrigerate for 4 hours or until chilled.

To serve, add half the crumble to a serving dish, spoon the pudding over it, and then evenly sprinkle the remaining crumble on top. If you wish to portion it out individually, divide it among 6 bowls instead.

YIELD: 6 SERVINGS

GOLDEE'S BANANA PUDDING CRUMBLE

In our early days, we were experimenting with homemade vanilla wafers for our banana pudding but never found a version that was flavorful enough. Eventually, we decided to blend store-bought wafers with butter, cinnamon, and salt, then layer the cookie crumbs on both the bottom and the top of each serving of pudding.

This method works, but Jalen was persistent, and eventually he came up with a homemade wafer recipe that is loaded with plenty of butter and cinnamon. This means you have to bake the crumble only once. While the cookies bake, your kitchen will become infused with the tempting scent of cinnamon, vanilla, and butter. You may notice that this recipe makes nine cookies and our pudding serves eight. That leaves an extra cookie for you as a cook's treat.

4 tablespoons unsalted butter, room temperature
6 tablespoons granulated sugar
2 tablespoons powdered sugar
1 large egg white
1 tablespoon vanilla extract
¾ cup (188 milliliters) all-purpose flour
2 teaspoons ground cinnamon
¼ teaspoon baking powder
½ teaspoon kosher salt
½ tablespoon whole milk

Preheat the oven to 350°F, and line a sheet pan with parchment paper.

Cream together the butter, granulated sugar, and powdered sugar until well blended. Stir in the egg white, vanilla extract, flour, cinnamon, baking powder, salt, and milk until well combined and a thick dough is formed.

Divide the dough into nine balls and place them evenly spaced on the prepared sheet. Gently press each cookie ball flat, and try to keep at least ¼-inch space between each cookie. Don't let them touch.

Bake uncovered for 14 to 16 minutes, or until the cookie edges are turning dark brown and the cookies are set.

Allow to cool for 20 minutes, then crumble the cookies with a rolling pin or your hands into small pieces and crumbs. (If you're hungry, take one of the cookies as a cook's treat.)

YIELD: 1 SHEET PAN OF CRUMBLE

BREAD PUDDING

Because we don't want to have any wasted food, our bread pudding evolved as a way to use up the heels from our loaves of bread. It used to be on the menu every day, but now we have only enough leftovers to make it once a week, on Sundays. Some people make the special trip just to be sure they get a portion of this limited treat. What makes it special is that we've kept it simple. It's the type of bread pudding recipe you could have found in your grandmother's recipe box.

The pudding itself is flavored with vanilla and molasses. To finish, we drizzle over it a vanilla glaze that's punched up with a splash of coffee or bourbon, depending on our mood. It's a rich and filling dessert, and while it's designed to be eaten warm, it can be enjoyed cold too. It can even be served for breakfast as its tender structure is similar to French toast.

FOR THE PUDDING

¾ pound (340 grams) white yeast bread
1 cup (250 milliliters) heavy cream
1 cup (250 milliliters) whole milk
4 tablespoons unsalted butter
3 tablespoons vanilla extract
½ cup plus 2 tablespoons (156 milliliters) granulated sugar
2¼ teaspoons molasses
¼ teaspoon kosher salt
3 large eggs

FOR THE GLAZE

2 tablespoons unsalted butter
1 tablespoon brewed coffee or bourbon
¼ cup (63 milliliters) brown sugar
¼ cup (63 milliliters) powdered sugar
¼ cup (63 milliliters) heavy cream
2 teaspoons vanilla extract
½ teaspoon kosher salt

Preheat the oven to 350°F, and lightly grease a 9-by-13-inch baking dish.

Rip the bread into bite-size pieces, and place them into a large mixing bowl. Pour the heavy cream and milk over the bread.

In a saucepan, melt the butter over low heat. Stir in the vanilla, sugar, molasses, and salt. Remove from the heat and allow to cool for 5 minutes.

Add the eggs to the butter, then whisk until well blended.

Pour the egg mixture over the bread, and mix everything with your hands until well combined.

Pour the bread mixture into the baking dish, cover with foil, and bake for 1 hour. Then remove the foil and bake until the top is lightly browned, about 15 minutes.

For the glaze, melt the butter in a saucepan, then stir in the coffee (or bourbon), brown sugar, powdered sugar, heavy cream, vanilla extract, and salt. Taste and make any adjustments you desire.

Pour the glaze over the cooked bread pudding, then serve warm.

YIELD: 8 SERVINGS

MANGO STICKY RICE

Nupohn and PJ grew up eating mango sticky rice as a special-occasion treat in their Laotian American home. This traditional Southeast Asian dessert is composed of tart, juicy diced mangoes layered on a bed of tender sticky rice rich with coconut cream syrup. To finish, we pour more coconut cream on top, then sprinkle on toasted sesame seeds for crunch.

Our preparation calls for pandan leaves, which impart a nutty, toasted flavor to the dish. You can source pandan leaves at Asian markets that specialize in Laotian or Thai ingredients, and they can be either fresh or frozen. If you aren't able to locate them, a little vanilla and almond extract will add a similar touch.

While our Lao Texas sausage (page 109) may contain a long list of spices and herbs, this dish's beauty is in its simplicity, which allows the fruit to shine. If you love rice pudding, mango sticky rice is for you.

3 cups (750 milliliters) cooked sticky rice (page 211)
1 13.5-ounce (383-gram) can coconut cream
⅓ cup (83 milliliters) palm or granulated sugar
½ teaspoon kosher salt
4 fresh pandan leaves, or ½ teaspoon vanilla extract plus ½ teaspoon almond extract
4 cups (1 liter) diced ripe mangoes
2 tablespoons toasted sesame seeds, for garnishing

If your cooked sticky rice is cold, gently heat it until warm either over low heat on the stovetop or in the microwave.

To make the coconut cream for the rice, stir the canned coconut cream, sugar, and salt into a saucepan until well combined. If using the pandan leaves, add those to the pan too. Over low heat, while stirring, cook the coconut cream until the sugar is dissolved and the cream is warm, about 5 minutes.

If using the pandan leaves, at this time remove and discard them. If you're not using pandan leaves, at this time stir the vanilla extract and almond extract into the cream.

Turn off the heat, and remove ½ cup of the coconut cream from the pan. This will be poured over the mango sticky rice like a syrup. It can be kept at room temperature if serving immediately or refrigerated and reheated later.

Meanwhile, add the warmed sticky rice to the remaining coconut cream on the stove and stir until the rice is well combined. Allow the rice to sit in the cream, uncovered, for 15 minutes so it can absorb some of the liquid.

To serve, top the coconut sticky rice with the mangoes, then pour the set-aside coconut cream over the mangoes. Sprinkle with toasted sesame seeds for garnishing.

We portion it out individually at the restaurant, though you can also serve it in one large dish and have people scoop out their preferred serving.

YIELD: 6 SERVINGS

Notes: Pandan leaves are similar to palm leaves, as they are pointed, narrow, and long. In Texas, the most common way to find them is frozen, and they'll be 1 inch wide and around 6 inches long. This size is what we recommend using. If your leaves are longer, you may cut them to size.

Canned coconut cream, like canned coconut water, is made with coconut and water. However, coconut cream has a higher fat content and is thicker and richer than coconut water, much like heavy cream is to skim milk. We don't recommend substituting coconut water for coconut cream in this recipe.

9 THE NEXT GENER

ATION

When you work at Goldee's, Lane will inevitably pose the question, "What is your barbecue concept going to be?" Whether you're standing at the kitchen service table trimming briskets, loading up logs onto the cart, or shaping bread, if there's a lull in the conversation, Lane will try to help you shape your personal vision for your ultimate barbecue tray.

Of course, we would love for the whole Goldee's family to stay together forever, but we know that some of us have big dreams we want to achieve, and we fully support that. While some restaurants prefer to scale by reproducing their concept over and over, we prefer to plant seeds instead. We give our team all the skills they need to go out and create their own barbecue dream.

For instance, when Lane worked with apprentice Zain Shafi, the two talked about Zain's culinary history and developed a menu that used Pakistani analogues for the classic Texas trinity of sides: potato salad, coleslaw, and beans. Zain also didn't eat pork, so he used sheep casings for his sausages and lamb for his ribs.

Chuck Charnichart's time at Goldee's was the same. She'd walk around with warm slices of her cinnamon swirl bread and a pink barbecue sauce she had created with smoked beets. We'd take the bread and dip it into the sauce, and the flavor combination was so wild that we knew her future restaurant would be very cool.

For over a year, Amir Jalali would travel six hours from Beaumont in Southeast Texas to Kennedale in North Texas. Despite the long drive, he always arrived carrying bags of cheeseburgers, biscuits, or fried chicken to share with the team. Amir thrives on being generous, and it's this nature that makes him a born restaurateur. Yet he's also a soulful cook, and when he shared a pot of his beans with the team, we fell in love with his cooking prowess too.

The rest of the team is no different. People may stay to learn as long as it's necessary to gain the skills they desire, but we would never try to clip anyone's wings. If they're ready to fly, we're happy to let them go and launch their own barbecue dream.

Since the writing of this book, Zain has opened a Pakistani-Texas barbecue trailer in Fort Worth. It's called Sabar, which is Pakistani for patience. It's a reference to both cooking barbecue, which requires much patience, and Zain's methodical journey from novice to pitmaster.

Chuck left North Texas for Lockhart and opened Barbs-B-Q. Her menu is a love letter to both her South Texas Mexican American roots and her travels around the world. As she learned how to cook, she spent time in Cairo and Oslo, places that have also inspired her menu. Yet despite the disparate influences, its cohesiveness has made Barbs an exciting place to visit.

Because Amir is so friendly and affable, he jokes that he's often underestimated. But underneath his warm demeanor lies a determined man who may be one of the hardest-working men in barbecue. He returned to his hometown of Port Neches, Texas, a small town in Southeast Texas. Inspired by his Persian, Cajun, and Italian roots, Amir produces a luscious tray that overflows with color, flavor, and passion.

As of this writing, Kim Ovalle is still at Goldee's. She has spent a few years working the pits, but her dream restaurant is a Texas-Mexican café, preferably in a cute Fort Worth house that's been transformed into a restaurant space. If it's anything like her, it will be warm, welcoming, and filled with a buzz of fun conversation.

Cecilia Guerrero has always gotten great joy from sharing food with others. Her sassy mind has come up with a barbecue concept name that is too racy to be printed here, but no matter what she chooses to do, it will be done with grace and deliciousness.

Joseph Bastian is still in college, developing more skills to complement his natural ability to make art. He can compose music, hand-letter a sign, or craft fantastic logos for his friends' endeavors. He has even helped us design some of our merchandise.

PJ Inthanousay has become an avid golfer. On his days off from Goldee's, you'll find him asking Jalen to play a round. Or he may book a trip to Japan to play the courses there by day and eat sushi by night.

Nupohn left us for a while, but we're very happy that he has returned. He's doing all the usual restaurant tasks, but he's also building out his Laotian barbecue dream menu for his concept called Dually's (which refers to the popular type of Texas truck that has double wheels but also to his dog).

Dylan is still in Colorado, herding animals and cooking over live fire. It's a peaceful life that suits him, and while we miss him in Kennedale, he comes back to see us some and we're just happy that he's found a life that suits him so well.

As for Jalen, Lane, and Jonny, they know that Goldee's is not something that can ever be re-created. But they wanted to try something new, and in 2024 they launched Ribbee's, a barbecue concept that focuses on baby back ribs. It's a simple menu composed of ribs, coleslaw, seasoned french fries, and a homemade roll. They designed it to be simple yet satisfying, and so far, this more chill concept has been well received.

We wish that everyone who worked with us would stay forever, but that's just not possible. If no one left, our little shack would get way too crowded. We miss having everyone here together, but we'll always be a family, and it's super cool to now have our friends opening restaurants across the state. Our dream of spreading Goldee's far and wide has come true. (And perhaps someday they'll share their creations in their own books!)

Now that we've shared our barbecue philosophy, method, and recipes with you, we hope you know that you're also the next generation. Cook for your loved ones! Do a pop-up concept with all your new ideas! Heck, maybe you also want to open your own restaurant. However you choose to celebrate cooking barbecue, please let us know so we can cheer with you. You, too, are the future of Texas barbecue.

GOLD SOUNDZ, A GOLDEE'S PLAYLIST

Here are some of the highlights of the Goldee's playlist. It's a cheerful mix of roots and pop rock from the middle of the twentieth century that is both rooted in the past and timeless enough to be fresh today.

"Everyday," **BUDDY HOLLY AND THE CRICKETS**

"Good Vibrations," **THE BEACH BOYS**

"This Will Be Our Year," **THE ZOMBIES**

"El Paso," **MARTY ROBBINS**

"Hey, Good Lookin'," **HANK WILLIAMS**

"All Day and All of the Night," **THE KINKS**

"Ring of Fire," **JOHNNY CASH**

"Mammas Don't Let Your Babies Grow Up to Be Cowboys," **WAYLON JENNINGS AND WILLIE NELSON**

"Turn! Turn! Turn!," **THE BYRDS**

"Oh, Pretty Woman," **ROY ORBISON**

"Happy Together," **THE TURTLES**

"Johnny B. Goode," **CHUCK BERRY**

"Jailhouse Rock," **ELVIS**

"I'm a Believer," **THE MONKEES**

"On the Road Again," **WILLIE NELSON**

ACKNOWLEDGMENTS

We're so thankful for all the people who helped us get our book into your hands.

First, we'd like to thank Casey Kittrell, our editor at the University of Texas Press. He took a chance on us, and his patience, persistence, and vision helped guide us as we completed our first book. Also at UT Press, we'd like to thank Robert Kimzey, Sarah Hudgens, and Derek George. We're so grateful for their hard work in taking our manuscript and turning it into a book.

We were incredibly fortunate to have an early version of our manuscript read by Adrian Miller and J. C. Reid. Their invaluable critiques and suggestions were much appreciated. It was also super cool to have two of our favorite historians and writers share their expert insights with us.

We'd also like to give appreciation for the enthusiastic home cooks who tested our recipes in their kitchens and backyards. Their valuable feedback guided us as we worked to translate our large-scale recipes into servings manageable for a home cook. Thank you to Beth Fain, Jay Fain, Ginny Heckel, Todd Heckel, Richard Jernigan, Lousie Kee, Susan McAfee Baxter, Katie Semple, Robin Street Morris, and Austin Zike.

Barbecue is meant to be shared, and when you're writing a cookbook, you have tons of leftovers. We'd like to extend a special shout-out to our team of hungry eaters who shared their opinions with us. Thank you Amanda Billings, Kevin Billings, Jeff Bourland, Karen Bourland, Cata Cooper, Chuck Cooper, Monica Crowley, Austin Fain, Chris Fain, Lisa E. Fain, Jacob Fain, Jonas Fain, Andrew Jernigan, Austin Jernigan, Hannah Emerson Jernigan, Julie Jernigan, Laura Kopchick, Alex Lewis, Shelley McKinley, Hillary Netardus, Catherine Osborne, Brad Sellers, Kevin Stephens, and Ann Tate. And a special thanks to Jean Jernigan and Wendy Adams Dominguez, two of this cookbook's biggest supporters who are no longer with us.

Our families and loved ones have been supporting us from the beginning, and we'd like to offer special thanks to them. Jalen would like to thank his parents, Jesse and Toni Heard; his brother, Aubrey Heard; his sister, Jennifer Cooligan; and his girlfriend, Shaya Mehdibeigi. Jonny would like to thank Jennifer White, Devon White, Carly White, and his grandparents Johnny "Pepaw" Lee and Vicki "Nana" Lee.

And from Lane: "Thank you to my mom and dad, Melanie and Chuck Milne; my girlfriend, Courtney Frederick; Will Milne for taking the beautiful pictures; Jalen, Jonny, Nupohn, and Dylan; the rest of my family and friends; Lisa Fain for writing the book and spending so much time; my puppy and kitties; all the people who have supported or will support Goldee's in any way in the future; and obviously all of the Goldee's staff, who help make Goldee's a special place every day. All of your support and encouragement made a huge difference. I am so grateful to have so much support behind me as I pursue my passion."

Lastly, we are so grateful for all of our customers and students. You inspire us to do our best every day!

BIOGRAPHIES

JALEN HEARD's grandmother wanted him to be a doctor, but he had other ideas. After working pitmaster stints at Freedmen's and Banger's in Austin, he decided to join his childhood friends in returning to his North Texas home to open their own barbecue spot. His calm nature, sense of humor, precision with knives, and attention to detail would have indeed served him well in a medical career, but the barbecue world is fortunate to have him too. When he's not working at Goldee's, you'll find him in his other role as the unofficial mayor of Fort Worth's Southside.

LANE MILNE has an incredible palate. He can take a bite of sausage, for instance, and ascertain what spices and meats were used, the ratio of liquid to solids, and how it was smoked. This culinary precision has served him well as he and his friends build their dream of spreading amazing barbecue throughout the world. Before opening Goldee's, he worked at Freedmen's and Micklethwait Craft Meats in Austin. He is a native Texan with family roots going back to El Paso on one side and England on the other. He spends his downtime experimenting with his true love, pizza.

JONNY WHITE is a risk-taker. While his gamble that getting a tattoo announcing the Atlanta Falcons Super Bowl win before the game did not pay off as he wished, after working in Austin at Valentina's and La Barbecue, his taking the leap to open his own restaurant has paid off many times over. He is a natural teacher and loves to share barbecue knowledge with anyone who will listen. When he's not tending the fires, you will find him in the Smash arena, most likely in the role of Kirby, who inspired Jonny's nom de barbecue, Jirby. You can also watch and learn from him on YouTube under that name.

LISA FAIN is the James Beard Award–winning creator of *Homesick Texan*, an online collection of recipes and stories celebrating Texan cuisine. She is also the author of several cookbooks, including *The Homesick Texan Cookbook*.

WILL MILNE is a commercial photographer and educator based in North Texas. He suffered through eating many pounds of delicious smoked meats to help bring this book to life.

INDEX

Page numbers in *italics* refer to photographs.